Stripping

INHERITED
KARMA

CRYSTAL WARBERG

BALBOA.PRESS

A DIVISION OF HAY HOUSE

Balboa Press books may be ordered through booksellers or by contacting:

Balboa Press
A Division of Hay House
1663 Liberty Drive
Bloomington, IN 47403
www.balboapress.com
844-682-1282

Print information available on the last page.

1 Corinthians 13:4-8 NIV
Scripture quotations marked NIV are taken from the Holy Bible, New International Version®. NIV®. Copyright © 1973, 1978, 1984 by International Bible Society. Used by permission of Zondervan. All rights reserved. [Biblica]

Interior Image Credit: Crystal Marshall

ISBN: 979-8-7652-4007-6 (sc)
ISBN: 979-8-7652-4008-3 (hc)
ISBN: 979-8-7652-4006-9 (e)

Library of Congress Control Number: 2023915009

Balboa Press rev. date: 08/21/2023

If an apology is empty, and in addition you're still repeating mistakes, you can't ask me to stop mentioning the past. If you offer me a sincere apology and change your behaviour, this is growth, and I'll never bring up our past issues again. The past is the present if nothing has changed, and from the present we continue to grow toward the future. There are only two options: growth or death. —Unknown

Contents

PART 3: THE FUTURE

Acknowledgements

Thank you to every being, living and passed, who has had a hand in giving me the courage and knowledge to step up and evolve to this point.

Thanks to Mom for the tough love and patience; Dad for the quiet guidance; Riley and my boys for helping me try and figure out what I want to be when I grow up; my blood sisters for all the tests that helped me learn to understand people—all of you, even the ones who won't read this book because you think I've lost my marbles!

Thanks to my soul sisters and yoga peeps for keeping me grounded. Thank you to my tribe of light workers, shadow workers, witches ... crazy loves company. It has been a universal effort, and continues to be, that gives me the courage to keep pushing forward and rise to my full potential.

Introduction

I'd never dream of going back in time. To change my past would change my present, and I would miss so many adventures.

When karma comes knocking, or in my case barking, you answer the door, or else she just gets louder! Since I was born under a Pisces sun/rising and Leo moon, it is no surprise that I would describe my greatest love as sleep. Here, without the obstacle of reality, the sky is the limit as to what I can do or have.

In September 2021, I said goodbye to Karma, my fifteen-year-old chihuahua-dachshund cross—my little girl I dressed in a Barbie coat and carried around in a pink faux-leather purse. I had fought with my husband for years to get my own purse puppy. Her death marked the end of one journey and the start of the next.

Bringing Karma into my life was a moment that feels like a lifetime ago. It feels like it was one of the last times I had the courage to go against what I was told to do and did something for me. So here I am. It's 4:32 a.m. on very dark December morning. *Wake up and answer the door,* Karma barks. This barking not audible to the average person, but then again, I'm not average.

I knew I was not meant to fit in. What I wish they'd taught in school was how to control my light so I could hide from those who would try to steal it.

Raised Roman Catholic, oldest of five girls, repression was my life. Dreams were my escape. I left home the first chance I got, and life took me on a few detours before I landed where I am now. While I intend to one day write about the beauty of transformation, this book is a realistic and messy look at the inner mind as I process and clean up generations of emotional patterns, inherited karma, and the resulting trauma.

Karma has to be cleared and healed before anyone can transform or experience conscious growth. Since high school, I've been collecting quotes from calendars, emails, and workplace newsletters. This was before the days of Facebook inspirational quotes, when I didn't even knew what an *affirmation* was. I started collecting quotes to motivate, inspire, and pull me out of some of the heavy ruts life tossed me into.

Unfortunately, after the first review of the book, I discovered that there is a lot of red tape in including copyrighted quotes, especially from dead people like Albert Einstein. Then it hit me: I decided to share my own story so that my words could hopefully support others. *My* words, not other people's quotes. I encourage you to listen to your heart and build your medicine cabinet of words to heal. Let your collection of words be greater than your collection of herbs and pills.

Every person, place and opportunity has the potential to become our greatest teacher.

There are ebbs and flows in life. If you ride the wave, listen to your intuition and make the changes necessary for you to grow. If you resist by limiting yourself to the tried and true methods, you're likely just reacting out of habit, and therefore progress can't occur.

As you ride the same wave over and over, the repetition starts to show in your body as dis-ease. We all either grow or decay. I'm realizing through clients as well personal experience that it often takes us staring mortality directly in the eyes before we take off life's safety belt. No belt means no safety of knowing the outcome. This still has the ability to paralyze me with fear.

However, I now know fear can motivate or debilitate. It is when I took off my safety belt that I reconnected to the reason I came to live this life. I hope that my story will encourage you to think big and realize you are stronger than you give yourself credit for.

When I was faced with kidney failure, I could have surrendered to society's expectations. Had I, I'm 99 per cent sure I'd have continued down the same path as my grandmother: popping pills, with dialysis in the near future. Instead, I woke up! I connected with the pictures in my mind of the future I wanted and the images that were on a loop in my current life. I realized I couldn't have both and set out to make changes.

I opened Pandora's box. It was so beautiful on the outside, I had to look in. But once it was opened, the surprises started flowing out, and growth became an addictive drug there was no way to stop. Each layer brought me closer to knowing what was at the bottom: my soul's gift to this world.

Through the difficulty, each challenge has made me happier and healthier. So many have to face a mortality wake-up before they make any changes. I'm hoping that if I step once more out of my comfort zone by being transparent and vulnerable, my readers will feel less alone and more supported in their efforts to find their life purpose or soul's calling.

Life is a series of cycles; there are ups and downs. Healthy support systems create a sense of safety, allowing you to surrender on the deepest level to the journey.

My mortality is what brought me to question my current beliefs. Doctors spend endless hours studying—and tens to hundreds of thousands of dollars in books and tuition—in addition to the countless numbers of patients they must see. The really successful professionals don't stop putting in their time when they physically punch out for the day. Doctors have spent the energy and money, and they are rewarded with what the current world values most: money and power.

Doctors have been granted a godlike position. So many people, including the old me, see a doctor as someone they must listen to—someone who knows all and sees all. However, in reality, doctors are really just well-educated guessers. Society has put them on a pedestal above the average human, but doctors are human too.

So what happens if doctors are wrong? Do they fall or fly? Just like me, many people seek the magic of energy work and explore their intuition only when doctors can't explain what is going on with their body.

I do support Western medicine. There are extraordinary diagnostic tools and treatments that can give patients more time to dig deeper and find the energetic reasons for their disease. Without medicine, I might not be here, so full respect to medicine and real science. While doctors have the tools to make the patient more comfortable, they're only putting a Band-Aid on the situation. The wound will continue to fester, and if the source of the disease is not removed, death is inevitable.

Blue pill or red pill? The red pill represents modern medicine—a quick fix to allow you to mask the discomfort and go one living life as you were. The blue pill resolves the source of the discomfort. But first you will learn unsettling and necessary life-changing truths. Which would you take?

Money was developed as a way to create universal exchange. First, we exchange our energy for money. We are not our own power source, so how do some continue to bleed cash beyond their energy output? How did we get to the point of creating such an imbalance in money and power between humans? The more money, the more power. How did a small percentage of the population earn the privilege to be worth more than others?

It's come to a point in society where we do need money to survive. A roof over our head and food in our belly will not manifest themselves. We no longer have access to many essential items, despite our reliance on the automobile, because so much is produced abroad. Where many see restriction, I see a challenge worth taking on.

Since I decided to follow my dreams and challenge my fears, my happiness has continually increased. Some of the richest people are the most miserable. Actors, musicians, the rich and famous followed their dreams because it was their passion. Take a look at all the celebrities again and notice how many have addictions. Their goal is no longer to follow passion; it is fame and the ability to make more money to maintain their star status. They get stuck on a hamster wheel due to the high they achieve from public acceptance.

Addiction is a form of self-medicating with anything in an attempt to lose oneself and return to that first high. Fame, money, food, alcohol, drugs, sex, and love are just some examples of addictions that will return the user to an ideal state of mind and emotion. It only takes one time of experiencing the high from an increase or suppression of energy and the user becomes drawn to use this substance each time they have the need to create a state of homeostasis.

This altered state is temporary. I can relate from watching as well as experiencing addictions with more socially acceptable substances.

Food is the most over used anxiety drug. Exercise
is the most undervalued antidepressant.

I've felt the push for a while now to write a book. I hated them growing up. I can still see my English 33 teacher rolling her eyes as she handed back a paper on a book I obviously never read but rather watched the movie. So when the idea first came to me to write one, I laughed at it.

I've journaled for years and written a few blogs. A few people over the years have told me that I have an ability to write—though not in a conventional, organized manner. As you will realize, my squirrels appear. My mind goes where the energy flows. I do seem to skip around, then out of nowhere a story appears, and I've made it full circle. We are not all the same. However, school attempts to mould us into clones.

Schools are not designed to support independent/creative thinkers but team players. They attempt to strip the individuality from children and young adults through discipline and competition. By the time they reach adulthood, all they are capable of doing is sitting down, shutting up, and doing as they are told.

Books have a lot of power if put in the right hands. History has shown us that those in power use censorship to control people. We send our children to locations to read from books that we their parents often haven't looked at beyond the cover. Our kids spend hours having their innocence, imagination, and individuality stripped. Governments and church bodies have outlawed, banned, and even gone so far as to have huge bonfires to burn books to keep them out of people's hands.

A man by the name of Klaus Schwab wrote *The Great Reset* and then sent a copy of his book to every world leader or person in a position of power. The book encouraged "global stakeholders to cooperate in simultaneously managing the direct consequences of the COVID-19 crisis. To improve the state of the world." I've purchased a copy, and it's on my to-read-this-year pile ... I think. Just holding it makes my skin crawl!

The decisions made by our government leaders as well as big corporations and pushed by government-paid media has resulted in a world divided. Parents like my husband have to choose between a medical procedure that has been identified as having side effects, including death, or putting food in his children's bellies. My son, who was on his way to championships for swimming, had to take a break and stop swimming because of this medical tyranny. I listened to my intuition. That gut feeling stopped me from putting a treatment which is now shown to have a high risk of causing cardiac diseases in young men and athletes, over folding to fear from a virus that he had *at least* once, possible three times so far, and had natural immunity.

The world shut down due to the ideas in Schwab's book. The plan in *The Great Reset* was to use a pandemic to require mandatory vaccination population control. This plan has already caused, through September 24, 2021, 812 cases of myocarditis and/or pericarditis in my province of Alberta alone (according to Alberta's provincial government website). In addition, there are many sources pointing to a significant upswing in total death numbers through the last two years.

With increases in deaths for all causes, the greatest killer now is a mysterious "unknown cause." Media normalizes strokes and facial paralysis in twenty-year-olds and SDS (sudden death syndrome) due to undiagnosed heart disease. Is this acceptance because of a book and elites with no medical background who we have put in power?

The good news is, our bodies are governed by a power greater
than any external force. All we need to do is be aware,
give our body the right tools, and heal. It's magic!

People in power pushing their agenda is not new. Long before Mr. Schwab's book, in 1604, an elite ruler by the name of King James commissioned a new translation of biblical scripture in 1604, as well as a compendium on witchcraft lore called *Daemonologie* (study on demonology). *Daemonologie* was the foundation to a follow-up book, *Malleu Maleficarum* (guide to hunting and interrogation of witches). These three books led to the prosecution, torture, and murder of millions of women. In some towns, every women was killed.

Today, the King James Bible is still used by religious individuals for their life guidelines. It entertains me that people I've known my entire life fear "the devil" has taken hold of me. They pray for my salvation. I welcome their prayers and am grateful for their love. Books of the past and present have forced humans to lower their frequency and sicken their bodies. Let this book be karma and help to bring things back in balance.

I was raised listening to stories about a man named Jesus who could turn water into wine. He transformed two fish into enough to feed an entire village. He made a blind man see. He rose to a position that made officials see him as a threat. He was crucified, died, and was buried. On the third day, he ascended to heaven. While I'm not expecting my stories to be as grand as Mr. J.C.'s, my journey hasn't been comfortable. I have learned to laugh through the tough times. I've shed more tears than I could measure. I experienced anger and its power to motivate.

I want you to see that you are stronger and more powerful than you give yourself credit for, just like I did. One passage I would love for my readers to track down is by Marianne Williamson. Google "Our Greatest Fear" or buy the book *A Return to Love: Reflections on the Principles of "A Course in Miracles."* It is one of my favourite audio clips I play to plant a seed at the end of my personal meditation/ savasana, or recite to empower students at the end of a yoga class.

This book is a reflection of how the events and people in my life made me feel through my shifts in consciousness. I remember reading a very fitting parable that describes why my stories may be different from how others experienced the same events:

> Five men were blindfolded and placed at various locations around an elephant. The first man, who was standing at the elephant's leg, was asked to describe what he felt. "It is tall, strong, and rough like a tree." The second man, located at the elephant's side, described the creature as "unmovable, like a wall." The third man, standing behind the elephant holding its tail, claimed it was a rope he held in his hand. The fourth picked up the trunk, sure it was large snake. The final man reached up, caressed the tusk, and identified the object as a pipe.

No one was incorrect or correct given the information their senses offered them. All parts were a fraction of a bigger picture (the elephant). My stories are only one part of the bigger picture. My stories have resulted from my experiences, lessons, setbacks, and growth.

I do believe people in my stories did not act out of evil or mean intention. They were just taking part in their own life journey, and our stories overlapped for a moment in time. The government gave me the time to think, write, and publish. When they made it illegal for me to teach yoga, and leave my country, they gave me the time to slow down and heal. I thank them for underestimating the power of a mom in a small Alberta town who will fight for her children and teach them not to lose faith in the power of love.

We live in a world where we rush our kids to grow up, then wonder why we don't know how to have fun as adults. The cycle stops with me!

The *past* is your lesson.
The *present* is your gift.
The *future* is your motivation.

Part One
THE PAST

Chapter 1

GROWING UP INDIGO

Peter Pan was on to something. I don't want to grow up!

Each time I'm told to write a bio, or a journey story, I find that the moment that got me to where I am keeps moving further and further back in my life. In my current location, I run a small yoga space where the majority of my income comes from one-on-one energy sessions. When I established there, my bio babbled on about my health crises and the loss of my dad. Despite his drinking and gambling, I declared myself a daddy's girl, and this woke me. Hence, the start of my journey to who I am today—blah, blah, blah. What a bunch of cut-and-paste bullshit!

If you don't believe every single thing that happens to you is part of a big plan for your best life, I challenge you to keep reading. Every detail was arranged, right down to your parents. My "bullshit" first bio is true and taught me a lot. However, the journey didn't start five days before my thirty-fourth birthday, when I experienced kidney failure, or a few weeks before my twenty-fourth birthday, when my dad died. It started long before I took my first breath, possibly lifetimes before I was even conceived.

And since that unknown time, so many adventures have built to this point. I am writing a book asking you to trust your intuition. You are part of something bigger than you could even imagine.

Indigo Children

The idea of an *indigo child* is not something new. In the 1970s, professionals and weirdo-hippie types started to notice there was a change in kids. A growing percentage of children being born had more energy, lower attention spans, higher IQs, and lower school scores despite their IQs. They were also more defiant. Doctors medicated many of these kids to make it easier for adults to rule over them, and gave them labels like ADHD, ADD, and LD.

The statistics show that the number of kids being prescribed pills has steadily increased over the years. Now more than half our children under twelve are on some sedative to control behavior. I noticed in the last couple of years a growing number of people my age (thirties and forties) who are close to me being diagnosed with ADHD and willingly being medicated. Most had less squirrelly brains than mine prior to choosing to be medicated.

I love my squirrels; they are part of who I am. When you do a coffee with me, despite that I've already switched to decaf, the conversation will never stay on topic. Before you know it, four hours will go by.

If you suspect you have ADHD, or have been diagnosed with a behavioral problem, I recommend you look for more information on the topic of indigos. Any of the books written by Lee Carroll and Jan Tober, I highly recommend. They include accounts from teachers, MDs, and psychologists, in addition to energy workers, on the misdiagnosis of indigos and medication that will do more harm than good. They do recognize that not every behavior diagnosis is due to someone being indigo, and that not every indigo will have behavior problems.

I give credit to my parents for having more kids than they could keep track of. It's probably why I slipped through the medical system. While many times I have wished for better focus, I have learned to love my messy mind and appreciate its ability to change channels if I don't like the show.

Clearing the Clutter

Yoga is not about touching your toes or contorting your body. That would imply competition and a final goal. Death is the end, and I don't think anyone is racing for death. Yoga is a way of life, a journey. It's creating space by clearing the clutter we have stored within our bodies by feeling the discomfort from the poses and acknowledging the experiences that come to mind along with the emotions we have not digested. Yoga creates space to plant new seeds and brings us back to the garden of Eden.

You are the best source of information about what is happening in your body. So do the work. Research, get outside suggestions, and most importantly, listen to your intuition—that wise one within. It comes down to a choice. Are you going to accept or question?

Accepting a diagnosis means accepting that your mind is broken, that it doesn't function correctly, that there is something wrong. This is an excuse! Instead, question everything and listen to the answers that pop into your mind. Sometimes the questions lead to more questions, but that's how we find the best answers, the best science. Humans can save humanity by doing their work and letting themselves see the change.

Enjoy the show that follows, because your increase in life (energy) does influence others, like moths to a light. Your frequency increase from loving yourself will draw people in who need change. Stop letting others control life—your life. It's your body, and you only get one per lifetime. It's time to take care of it.

Consuming pills to quiet your mind so you can work more, make more, or sleep less will only wear you out. You chose not to fit into societal norms as part of your life plan. So now it's time to figure out why.

My research helped me understand that I wasn't as alone as I thought. I am one among many. I find it ironic that a similar amount of people—an estimated 10 per cent of children born between 1970 to 1980—are suspected of being indigo. It was also an estimated 10 per cent of the population that refused to follow the Canadian government's mandates. The drama teacher running Canada assumed it was just this disobedient portion of citizens who were making their way to Ottawa. He called it "a small fringe minority, with unacceptable views." This fringe minority resulted in a convoy that inspired the whole world. We are evolving, and it's time humanity evolves too.

Sometimes it feels easier to disassociate, escape to your imagination of the past, or make believe. To make the assumption that you're not from this planet—an alien, a star seed—or that you've spent more time in a different dimension/planet and want to go home. Perhaps you'd prefer to suppress, self-medicate, and avoid growth. You have a choice: wait out your time (like a prison sentence) until the day comes for your earth parting, or face the facts that you are here and chose to be here for a reason, and do the job you came here to do!

The first generation of indigos were born to push society's norms and expectations—to break the systems of society so that the following generations could build a better one. The first wave of indigos are currently in their forties and fifties. These are our managers, recognized doctors, established lawyers, and senior teachers. We are now the ones at the top of the food chain, the ones with the greatest power to educate and support the even more energetically evolved humans coming up behind us. But first, we must repair the trauma from the generation before us. We must steady the ground to allow for a strong foundation.

When it's a requirement of the soul,
I choose to ask for forgiveness rather than permission.

Chapter 2

GENETIC KARMA

I chose my parents so that they could show me where they went wrong. Wish it didn't take me so long to listen. Dad says, "Better late than never!"

A large part of my healing journey was discovering who my parents were, because their journey was as much a part of my journey as it was theirs. It is said that a daughter looks for her father in her husband and that a son looks for his mother in his wife. While I loved my dad and would even go as far to say I was a daddy's girl, I can say with confidence that I did not want to marry a man like my father.

My parents met while they were in their teens. Mom was 16 and a waitress at a gas station restaurant off the highway. Dad was a cute two-time high school dropout with a nice smile. He went to work for an oil and gas company instead of receiving his diploma. From the stories I've heard from both of them, it was instant attraction. They were both kids looking for love; however, neither one actually had experienced or knew what unconditional love was.

They did what every young, emotionally traumatized child does: they fell in lust, put up with each other's baggage, broke up, reconnected a time or two, and eventually got married. The hope in those days was to get hitched before any kids were conceived. No living together or children before they got married. They succeeded!

I did hear about some of the hard times in their relationship. Some Mom had moved past, or so she thought. I don't believe she really processed or came to terms until she revisited them while she helped me do some healing over the last few months.

Dad lived the oilfield life, drinking excessively, and resentment grew as his roles and responsibilities shifted. With each daughter, he moved further and further from having the ability to live a selfish life. The expectation was to surrender his freedom to his growing family's needs. Dad was a textbook Scorpio—he had emotions greater than anyone I've ever known, yet the inability to digest or reflect on them due to his astrological and genetic birthright.

Mom was lonely raising kids. I feel she grew resentful that she had to share her time when Dad was home with a growing number of little ladies. There were many opportunities for the two of them to grow and change the cycle within their relationship. But nothing changed between them. He continued to drink. He lost jobs, his licence, our home. She continued to have faith that he would turn over a new leaf.

Mom eventually went back to high school, completed her nursing degree, and got a job at the local hospital. A few years later, Dad passed away of cancer. They never had the opportunity to work past their trauma—to fall out of love, grow, and then rekindle love with a mature heart.

I do believe two people who have grown apart can reconnect. When they do, without the damage from old family trauma, they will come from a place of authenticity rather than expectation. Their bond will be stronger than ever imagined. Two people who can see the world through each other's eyes and support each other's dreams for the future without forcing each other's beliefs are an unstoppable force of God power.

It is human to seek out that which completes us: connection after a lifetime of conditioning through division. The day we realize that we contain all that we need—there is no separation, we are connected to all—then and only then does the loneliness go away and we can honour another individual soul's journey. This is the place of mature love.

Father Wound

A father's job is not to teach his daughter how to be a lady. It's to teach her how a lady should be treated.—Unknown

While Dad was alive, and now that he is gone, he taught and continues to teach me exactly what I needed to know in a very quiet way. In a sense, while he was alive, he steered me away from males like him, and if I saw any inkling of a trait my father shared in common, I flipped on the very natural passive-aggressive charm and ghosted them. First impressions only: no one who had an unsatisfied thirst for alcohol, no one voicing an interest in pipeline or equivalent employment. An overly athletic male was the biggest red flag, because I wanted a smart partner, not a pretty one.

When Dad was home, he showed up for us girls, and I assumed that was just what dads did. Nobody to my knowledge was divorced or a single mom. As a kid, it was plausible to assume that moms did the raising and dads did other things outside the home like working. I was shielded, and we didn't talk about my dad's poor behaviour when or after he had been drinking.

Pony-back rides and '60s music dance parties in the living room were highlights of the times when Dad was home. The other stuff, like me climbing into my sister's bed because of the yelling, and the knowing after one of those loud nights why there was another hole in the wall or a comatose father with a black eye on the living room floor, was normalized and not talked about. As I got older, I knew this was not how a husband should treat his wife.

I knew I would never marry, or even enter a relationship, with someone who excessively drank. I felt I had a sound system to avoid this. My plan was to pick a smart guy. I figured if he was smart, he wouldn't become a oilfield employee, and problem averted.

As the oldest of five, I felt like I was parenting my younger sisters. I was dealing with kids all the time as a kid, so I had no intention of children. Especially since I didn't foresee a partner being an active participant in raising kids. In fact, there were many characteristics I overlooked. I was focused on the surface characteristics: career and habits. No acknowledgement for why people behaved the way they do or that they had an ability to change.

There is no perfect *one* because we all have unhealed trauma that makes us act irrationally from time to time. We are all here to live, grow, and heal through our entire life. The man I chose has taught me a lot of lessons. The important thing that I did not realize until I was writing this book is that a partner needs to be able to communicate—to listen, respect, and express. A partner must be able to see past the social judgments and expectations and trust that the other person's fears are warnings that something needs to change.

Discomfort, including in a relationship, signals an opportunity for growth. Untreated discomfort leads to dis-ease, leaving only two outcomes: change together or grow apart.

My parents decided to take over my father's father's store in a nearly empty town called Robsart in Southern Saskatchewan. Without a high school diploma or a licence, my father's job prospects were limited. Mom hadn't completed high school either, and they were both of the mindset that the man brought home the bacon while the wife cooked it and cleaned the greasy pan after.

At this time, the head count of little ladies to feed was four. Grandpa was looking to retire, and my parents needed a fresh start. So they exchanged residences plus some cash, and Dad moved back to the community in the middle of nowhere. While some felt this wasn't a fair trade, I know that this was exactly what needed to happen. Here he could reconnect with some of his old-time friends and have an opportunity to revisit his past and heal.

But instead, the drinking and poor choices continued. I was 10 when we moved. At this age, I was starting to recognize patterns and make sense of the first whispers about Dad's upbringing. Fast forward a few years, add another little lady, and the store was forced to close. We moved back to Alberta, where Dad continued to drink.

There was a lot of growth that happened from our move to Robsart. Not everyone sees the change as positive, and our extended family did fracture. But I do believe that when we refuse to grow, the universe steps in. The universe, God, Mother Earth—it is undeniable that there is a higher power, and when we refuse to grow or change our patterns, it steps in and forces us. Sometimes the change is subtle. Other times, it's a kick in the ass that sends a person and those around them into a tail spin for an extended period of time.

When the store closed, my parents had lost everything except us five girls. I was just completing Grade 7 at the time, and due to the bullying that was happening, I couldn't leave soon enough. While I experienced the minor discomforts of peer pressure, my father was put in a position between his wife and family, a place karma would later give me the opportunity to experience and learn from.

Robsart gave my dad closure to his childhood. I believe he realized that my mom loved him unconditionally, which was why he chose her over his family. Unfortunately, he never learned to deal with the trauma from his family abandonment. The emotions continued to fuel him, and he continued to self-medicate with alcohol. This discomfort led to disease and finally his death. But that wasn't where his teaching stopped. In the last couple of years, Dad has reached out and continued to teach me. More to follow in coming sections on my present and future.

We choose our parents as much as our parents choose us. We are each other's greatest teachers, bound together by blood. A son is made in the image of a partner who would be ideal for his mother.

She seeks to create that which she wishes she had. This is why a son looks for a partner in his mother's likeness.

A daughter can do no wrong in her father's eyes. He may disagree with her choices, possibly even voice his concerns, but he will eventually discover there is no way to tame her unless he breaks her. In a healthy paternal relationship, a father will always choose, if given a choice, to stand by his daughter, protect her, and provide safety while she finds her place. It is this safe place that a daughter seeks in her partner.

Mother Wound

Life doesn't come with a manual. It comes with a mother.—Unknown

It wasn't until I became a mom that I discovered how invisible being a mom makes you feel. You dedicate every cell of your body to making, raising, and protecting this little creature, and in turn, they go away and create a life that has very little to do with you. This is how it's supposed to be! As mothers, we give them the tools to grow. We need to support them in a way that *they* need. We are there to help them get back up when they decide to do it their way and fall. Moms don't always have the answers, but they have experience to share, ears to listen, and love to heal the pain from life's lessons. Thank you, Mom, for being you.

My mom was the oldest of five, like me. She grew up with less than the average income, like me. The standard of living has improved from her generation to mine; however, I do feel that we had economically similar upbringings when looking at the standard of living for our times. Mom shared a bed with her siblings until the day she married, and then she shared a bed with her husband. Just like me ... well, almost. I was expected to share a bed, but I carried my sister, twelve years younger than me, to the couch most nights once she fell asleep.

Mom suppressed, and medicated with cigarettes, food, and alcohol. She would find a vice to cope with life. Just like me! I remember Mom with her exercise programs growing up, whether it be videos or a stationary bike. There were periods my sisters and I knew to stay away or feel her wrath, as she would surrender one vice for another.

She was taught at a very young age that things that cause conflict or confrontation need to be ignored. Children are very resilient; however, if they do not have a role model supporting their spirit, they never learn healthy ways to react, talk, digest, and regulate emotions. This results in poor and unhealthy patterns to be repeated through adulthood. The longer someone is stuck in those patterns, the more resistant to change they become. The energy literally becomes toxic, and disease in the body sets in.

While I loved my grandmother (and Mom claims I was one of her favourites), I wish she could have know then what she learned later. It would have made my growth so much easier. Grandma Josie discovered in her thirties that her kidneys were in very bad shape. Energetically, kidneys are associated with retention of resentment. She too was the oldest. She married a man (my grandfather John) many years older than her.

She was very much an extrovert. I learned this through the time I spent sleeping in her spare room through high school to escape the responsibilities of home. Living and raising children in the middle of nowhere, with no transportation, was not a heathy environment for someone like my grandma.

Grandpa got very sick, and Grandma ended up raising my younger uncles more or less on her own. She cleaned hotel rooms and houses to earn a little income. When Grandpa died, I remember her doing a little travelling before her health prevented her from living her fullest life possible. She regularly had card nights, which I did attend and got to see her with her people, and not just as *grandma*. Josie was a big lady in both personality and stature. She had a few vices that she used to medicate herself, and eventually the undigested resentment led to total kidney failure. Finally, the extra strain led to heart failure.

The evening she passed, I was suppose to visit and fix her sewing machine. In a spontaneous decision, I decided to stay home, and coincidentally conceived my third child. There were three weeks of guilt before I discovered one more was going to join our family. For me, regret led to a lesson in how everything happens in its time. The past is gone, no regrets—things happen when they are supposed too. For me, what better reason than to receive the third baby I really wanted?

Each Mother Would Like to Say

A year has gone,
My child has grown.
A lot of thanks to Mrs. Joan.
I regret to see the time go by,
Snatching moments as they fly.
Learning from such little steps,
I had to feel not so inept.
The time, it comes, as mothers say,
To pass the torch another way.
This woman took the hand from mine,
She smiled and said it would be fine.
As history repeats itself,
I watch my precious grow.
And as the time was spent,
A bond was made; a promise kept.

—Linda Warberg
Written in 1985 by my mother when I went to kindergarten

Chapter 3

MY BEGINNING

It grows, it blossoms, and lives its life where God planted it. Of little prominence, yet fulfilling its purpose. All the while hoping to be greater. It doesn't realize someday it's seeds will be released and impact the whole world ... Dandelions.—Unknown

I was born under a waxing gibbous Leo moon. It was literally written in the sky the emotional and lonely journey this life would be. *Waxing gibbous* indicates that this life journey would be more independent—not necessarily that I would be alone, rather that the responsibility would be mine. I had to learn to trust my intuition in regard to what is needed to live my highest and best life.

As a Leo moon, I am enthusiastic, proud, loyal, spontaneous in my decisions, and seeking to be a leader. The majority of the planets were located above the horizon and to the left, which shows that I am outgoing and tend to be more of an extrovert, with the tendency to be more independent and self-motivated. I was born to be a master of my own destiny.

With more than half the planets located in the cadet house, my placements show that I was born with the ability to see an entire situation rather than concentrating on just the individual parts.

Analyzing is my jam; however, follow-through is tricky because I never feel I have all the evidence. This is the sole reason I started to write my story. I need to organize my thoughts, limitations, growth, fears, and possible futures. I often use my experiences to help others, so I thought perhaps the energy I put into this book would help someone else. I did not expect it to help me with clarity to the extent it did.

I heard of the term *indigo child* many years ago, and in a day when everyone wants a label, this one felt very natural. *Loves animals*, check: I have a house full. *Extremely empathic*, check: I have lost count of the number of times I've called or messaged someone when they needed to talk. My empathy goes beyond time and space. *Not part of the social norm*, huge check: 100 per cent not normal.

As I decided to reconnect with my authentic self, I became aware of just how not-normal I am. *Normal* is the same as *average*. Society make assumptions on people based on the average or norm. Only thing someone can assume about me is you never know what the outcome will be. This makes people uncomfortable. I'm okay with this, because I've realized this is a gift not a curse to make people uncomfortable. My ability makes me a great teacher, encouraging people to grow. It's their choice as to whether to take part or fear me. The discomfort I bring about, in my experience, is due to something within them they have repressed or are inspired to embody (jealousy).

Home is where I was born, in Medicine Hat, Alberta, 1979. I've left a few times but always made my way back. In the healing community, many say that until you've learned everything you need from a place, it will keep calling you back. Maybe this is why when people come, they tend to never leave.

I attended a Catholic elementary school, up until midway through Grade 5. I had a couple of close friends, and a best friend who I met in Grade 2. Candace and I even kept in contact for a few years after we moved, but lost touch when we moved back to Alberta. Our dance routines are special memories created while living on Cameron Road. For the most part, a pretty normal period of my life.

As I mentioned earlier, Mom stayed home, and Dad was away lots. When he'd come home evenings before bed, we would horse around and dance in the living room. Often, hours after we had climbed into bed, my parents would start arguing. I'd climb into my sister's bed to comfort her. It made time go by faster during their fights.

When our rooms were moved to the basement with the coming of two more sisters, I welcomed the space. We had toys and our imaginations to take us places, or bring to life creatures like monsters and unicorns to pass the time.

Technology has made imagination and independent thought, in general, obsolete. We simply push a few buttons or make a voice command, and a tiny box allows us to escape to another's reality. By adulthood, our imagination/thought muscles have been so underused that it is nearly impossible to access them. When we don't use a muscle, it eventually becomes useless. This practice has made it impossible for so many to "think outside the box."

I am pretty sure I remember the night Dad was caught drinking and driving. It was my sister Amy's birthday sleepover. This dream or memory revisits me often: me half asleep and Mom telling me she had to go get Dad. It was shortly after that we moved to Saskatchewan.

I dream in first person for the most part, so it's sometimes its hard to tell the difference between dream (imagination), reality, and more recently, what some would call psychic/prophet dreams (potential futures). I'm pretty sure that evening was a universal course correct—an attempt by something bigger to break my parents' cycles. Some would see it as unlucky that the check stop had been set up in that spot after Dad chose to have a few drinks and then get behind the wheel, a choice he had made many times before. Luck, or was it karma catching up and attempting to force change?

This change of course didn't just affect my dad. It would attempt to put my entire family back on our life track. Once again, though, Dad chose to fall into old cycles.

Free will is the right gifted by God, and the foundation that all other rights and freedoms are based on. Each choice has a result. Unfortunately, it doesn't always keep us in Eden.

Chapter 4

ROBSART THEN

A soul place is where we go when we close our eyes. You are drawn to this place like a treasure map. It's the place that allows you to heal, grow, and find the purpose of your soul's journey. It's real. Go find it!

It seemed to happen overnight. When I talk to my mom about the decision to take over the store in Saskatchewan, it wasn't well thought out. It was absolutely a case of Dad listening to his heart and not their heads.

Grandpa stuck around for a little bit while things transitioned to the change of ownership. I remember my parents making their mark on the business with the removal of the raised office, and relocation of the post boxes. Amy and I from time to time would try to help by scrubbing the nine-by-nine tiles and bringing a fresh clean look to the previously white-speckled surface. We only made it a few rows before we discovered that this was a losing battle, and were granted permission to go explore the town.

Robsart was founded in 1906, and my great-grandfather was one of the Norwegian farmers who came out to these Canadian badlands to start a life of promise. The land was hard, the wind was strong, and the water was scarce. But with the help of the rail line, the town had a good start. It maintained itself through the bootleg days.

As a Redcoat town, it was a stopping place for rum-runners. Unfortunately, it was fire after fire, in addition to the growing reliance on personal automobiles, that led to its final demise. While we lived there at the end of the '80s transitioning into the '90s, there were still a few stable buildings. Today, it is littered with abandoned vehicles and structures that are one good windstorm away from returning the land to its natural barren field. It is, for lack of better words, a ghost town.

Ghosts. I have always believed in them. As I was raised Catholic, they weren't discussed much, because we were taught that when you died, you went to one of two places: heaven or hell. One day while watching a movie, which we did often, I heard the term *purgatory*. I'm not sure what movie it was, probably some B-list, never-made-it-to-theatres horror movie. My parents also provided movie rentals to supplement the store's income. One of the perks was we often watched movies that were definitely not age-appropriate.

I remember watching the *Child's Play* movies when we got them in. Shortly after my sister locked her Cricket doll in Mom's chest, the key mysteriously disappeared. For the record, I did see her eyes roll and her mouth open from time to time, despite us removing her batteries, so it was a necessary move.

Purgatory is a place where lost souls go. They either didn't fit into either of the other two mentioned; died suddenly so didn't realize they were dead; or died before their time. One reason or another, they simply didn't cross into heaven or hell. The idea of purgatory brought a level of comfort and perhaps an explanation as to why I could feel people around as my sister Amy and I explored Robsart. I could *feel*, but when I looked around, there was no body.

When I was a child I was afraid of ghosts. As I grew up
I realized that people are more scary.—Unknown

To some extent, I've blocked the time I spent in a Saskatchewan school. Classes were very small and always split. My only memories are of mean girls. They would be friends with me one moment and threaten to beat me up the next. I had a cousin my age, and I'm pretty sure he was just as scared of them as I was.

Grade 7, I excelled academically, probably more out of spite than actually caring about school. This is something I did throughout my school years. I could play the pretty dumb girl, but there were times it was fun to excel and put someone in their place. Grade 7 was one of these years.

In school at this time, if you placed in the top percentage, you didn't have to write finals. My cousin was super-smart, and the queen mean girl usually measured up pretty close to his grades. That year, I managed to reach what I felt were genius levels in everything but language. This made the queen bee extra-mad.

When grades were posted, things got so heated, I started having to hide out in bathrooms and book council appointments to avoid a confrontation on breaks. Eventually, I took a leave for the last few days, only returning when my dad drove me to town for my exam. We left once school was out for the summer, and I never looked back until the summer of 2017.

We have been educated into believing we must audition for the lead role. Life has become about division instead of progression. We are trained so we learn that we are individually responsible to set the bar, not only for our success but to lead the way for generations to come. We are told only the smartest, prettiest, and most athletic will receive monetary proof of success. The rest have already failed. Failure according to the current system means our dreams cannot be accomplished. What is not realized is that from the ashes of one man's seed rises success.

Robsart was a place of hopes and dreams for my great-grandfather. It was the place my grandfather made his mark in the history books, operating the general store. It's where my parents hoped for a fresh start and had dreams of opening a B & B. My great-grandparents planted the seed. My grandparents and parents nourished the dream. Karma has brought me back and lite a spark.

My time in Robsart was filled with mixed experiences and emotions. I've always been a prairie girl. It's sunsets are what my dreams are made of. Will I also fertilize the seed of a community in nowhere Saskatchewan? Or will I be the Warberg who makes it happen?

Chapter 5

JACK AND DIANE

I'm not perfect. I'll annoy you, say stupid things.
But I'll always love you.—Unknown

In May 1991, my parents welcomed another daughter, bringing the count to five girls. The store was unable to compete with urban markets, so it closed permanently that year. I remember Dad making trips to Medicine Hat and filling coolers with milk and ice cream because it was cheaper to haul them in himself than pay the trucks to deliver to his small rural general store.

Dad had started doing more labour to cover expenses and grasping at opportunities to keep us in Robsart. He also did a lot more socializing, which included drinking. He seemed happy when he was out doing his thing, and I felt blessed to be able to tag along. Perhaps it was because the alternative was being home, where I'd be bossed around and made to help with my younger sisters, including the baby. Or perhaps Dad had lessons he needed to teach me about slowing down and priorities before his early departure.

One of the projects Dad had going on was the relocation of what was to be Mom's dream home. This is where they could grow old together and continue to operated a B & B once us kids grew up and left home.

I wish I could see my dad's whole astrology chart; however, knowing that his sun was in Scorpio explains a lot. Scorpio sun placement can influence and make a person very passionate, but they don't know how to communicate these intense feelings, so they tend to suppress them. I suspect the suppression occurs for a few reasons:

1. Scorpios feel their feelings generally more than other people. Controlling their feelings is kind of like diffusing an ignited explosive: dangerous and messy.
2. They are highly empathic, and so they often are experiencing other people's feelings in addition to their own. Most Scorpios, I suspect, may not even be aware of the outside influences and take ownership for all the emotional energy they are experiencing. This can cause additional confusion in communication.
3. They have a saviour complex and have this need to protect those they care for. Feelings for most Scorpios makes them vulnerable, something they avoid at all costs.

Dad loved Mom, but due to the way he was raised, he never knew how to express any of his feeling, aside from anger. Anger, I suspect, was not something he willingly expressed; rather, one he couldn't contain.

Dad had so many hurdles to overcome. It did not work out to his advantage being a male born in the '50s, a time when emotions were seen as feminine. He wasn't raised in a stable home but rather passed around redneck country while his mom was institutionalized and his father struggled to organize and raise eight kids. With such intense emotion and no guidance on releasing it, he fell into social circles that normalized drinking.

Dad told me on many occasions that he was drinking regularly by age nine and smoking by twelve. When we don't have the support and knowledge, sometimes unknowingly the wounds we experience become so deep that full healing takes more than one lifetime. For this reason, I am happy to work with my dad clearing out some karma to help lighten the load for the next go-round.

Within two and a half years of our move to Robsart, the store went broke and my parents welcomed my youngest sister into the world. They packed up what they could in their vehicles, and we once again started over. We left more than just a few toys and cars in Robsart. We left a big piece of my dad, which I would find when I returned in 2017.

Our first stop was Irvine, Alberta. It was a three-bedroom house, two up, a partial finished basement with one down. We lived there for two years—a rest stop for my parents. Mom returned to school, Medicine Hat College, to get her high school diploma. Dad attempted to get his mechanics papers through the college and apprenticed at a small highway garage/gas station in Irvine.

Unfortunately, tragedy struck, and all Dad's tools went up in a garage fire. He defaulted back to the oil and gas field. Personally, I don't think his heart was in getting a piece of paper that said he was a mechanic. The man had been ripping apart vehicles since he was a child. I find it hard to believe he would have been happy sitting still listening to some man talk in a classroom or correct him in something he loved to do. I think he was just trying to gain some credibility with the world after a few mess-ups.

Mistakes can sometimes create the best memories.

I don't have a lot of memories of the time in Irvine. When I was there, I had my first few boyfriends and learned that not everyone kissed the same. Some were very sloppy. I learned to laugh at and push the envelope of what is socially acceptable. I never did the pimply adolescent. I went from child to young woman overnight.

My youngest sister was twelve years younger than me. Unfortunately for my parents, I did not look 12. With my blonde hair and curves, I attracted a lot of attention from the older boys in the small rural school I attended. I often would watch school sports, where I could crush on all the older boys who gave me the attention I so desperately wanted.

Because Mom needed help, I'd have to babysit. So, multi-tasking, I'd pack my baby sister on my hip and giggle at the judging eyes who assumed my sister was my own child. Girlfriends were few, but boys were plenty.

One friendship I would make was with a guy I meet at a volleyball game from another rural school, Schuler. We talked from time to time, but in those days, everywhere rural was considered long-distance, so it was expensive to carry on a long-distance friendship. Tucker would be one of my closest friends in the coming years, and he helped me through some really tough times.

In the summer after I finished Grade 9, we moved back to Medicine Hat. It had been less than five years since we left, but it felt like a whole different world.

Chapter 6

THE RETURN

The caterpillar shows us that beautiful things happen when we find rest within darkness. Caterpillars don't wake up one morning transformed. They have to lock themselves away and become a squishy mess. Five to twenty-one days later, they have to fight to re-enter the world. Without the caterpillar's commitment to change, we wouldn't see the beauty of its sacrifice.

Prior to our move to Saskatchewan, we lived in a house my parents owned from new, which they bought shortly after they married. With ownership came pride for my dad, and the house was well cared for. Dad had built a huge garage, and together they decorated the home according to modern decor.

Moving back to Alberta and starting over was a hard transition. They had to rent, first in Irvine and once again when they returned to the city of Medicine Hat. Renting a place that would fit a family of seven couldn't have been easy; however, they did find a multi-family home near the local high school that I was to attend for the balance of my high school education. Instead of going back into the Catholic system, where I would have reconnected with some of my elementary friends, it was decided to put me in public school.

Moving back to the city was bittersweet. I no longer had to deal with the country cliques that I did not fit in with. Both Robsart and Irvine were not very welcoming to the new kid. Or perhaps it was just because it was the awkward teen years.

Living back in the city allowed my mom easier access to the amenities she needed to run the house smoothly. In addition to college and child care for my youngest sister, Dad was able to return to work in the oil and gas field due to the relationships he had developed over the years. Instead of being gone fracking for extended periods, he was working more in the shop and was home a lot more.

I had my first job at the dry cleaners across the alley, a boyfriend, and a social life of my own. Life was good! With Dad's extra cash flow, there were more luxuries and dreams being discussed between he and Mom. There was also more socialization and drinking.

I don't recall the date, but what happened after my parents returned from a night out will always be one of my core memories. I know it was shortly after my sixteenth birthday. I was given a daughter's pride, which I had been hoping for years to get.

I believe they had gone to an Easter/Spring breakup party, a common practice with pipeline and oilfield workers. I was between boyfriends and having a normal rant with Tucker about how much guys suck. I was home keeping an eye out while my sisters all slept.

Then came the yelling. The words were a blur, but the language was charged. Us kids knew just to lay low and eventually the storm would settle. Tomorrow Dad, if not both my parents, would need to sleep it off.

I got off the phone with Tucker when I heard something smash. Enough was enough! I don't recall Mom ever being struck, and I can say without a doubt Dad had never lifted a hand to us kids— with the exception of a spank, which was probably within socially acceptable reasons of the time. It was a standing joke that when we did something wrong, we'd want a spanking from Dad, because we knew it hurt him more than it hurt us. Walls and other objects were the stuff that took the blows from his temper.

I loved both my parents, but when they got like this, I couldn't understand why they were still together. I wished that they would just divorce! I decided to come to Mom's rescue and charged out of my room.

The wall between the living room and dining/kitchen was a cabinet with glass shelves. I could see Mom turn as I assessed the glass not from the shelves but from one of her lampshades that had been shattered into a million pieces throughout the unit and all over the kitchen.

"I'm calling the cops!" I said. Then I raced back to my room.

Dad reached my room just seconds after I did, but it was too late: the operator was already on the line. Dad grabbed the wrist that was holding the base of the phone while the other hand had the receiver to my ear. He squeezed tight but didn't say a word. Words could not describe what I saw in his eyes.

He let go and went to his gun case. Humiliated by his actions, he told Mom that "the world and we would be better off without him."

Mom cried. Dad left on foot, leaving his gun behind. Mom then came to my room pleading that Dad was a good man, and he loved me. She begged for forgiveness for him.

At the time, I was confused more than anything—not scared, mad, or sad. This event took place because it was supposed to. It was why I chose to become part of this family—my mother's daughter, my sisters' protector, my father's teacher. I came here to break the cycle, to stop karma from repeating itself.

There were a few awkward weeks, maybe a month, where Dad lived in a motel a couple blocks away. I wasn't able to see him because of the restraining order and court stuff. But he let me know he loved me and that he was sorry with some roses and a small card. The flowers obviously died, but that card still sits in my "daddy box."

Mom refused to press charges, so the officers and the court charged him with improper storage of his firearms. I remember both my parents being mad and saying that they didn't have to charge him. The funny thing is, yes they did! Once again, when you ignore the signs, the universe (God) steps in and tries to force you back on track. Each time my parents resisted, the force just got more aggressive.

Shorty after Dad was free to come home, my parents decided to start over *again*. Dad stopped drinking; this time it just changed to slot machines. The house they picked was located on an acreage just outside Medicine Hat. There was a collection of homes with a sign that said City View Estates. We had a fair-sized ranch-style home, blue in colour, on a three-ish acre lot. It was big enough that my parents said we could have a pony, but the selling feature was definitely the triple-car garage.

There were only three bedrooms, so that meant I would have to share again, and it wasn't fully finished. Large pieces of teal-green carpet covered the concrete ground, and the kitchen cupboards had no doors. The house was a big project, but my parents felt it had a lot of potential.

They quickly discovered that they had bitten off more than they could chew. The house was permitted to be a garage, and my parents would spend years in court trying to get retribution for the loss of value to the property, and all the repairs they would have to do to bring the structure up to code. Once again, my parents' spontaneous fresh start landed them in a financial loss.

It was the summer we moved to the acreage that I would fall in love for the first time. It was love at first sight. We put up with each other's baggage, broke up, and reconnected, but for us it never ended in marriage, just a lot of lessons. My sisters all returned to urban school, where I spent my last two years, hitching a ride with my mom to town.

By this point, Mom was in the nursing program at the college, and my youngest sister was in preschool. The days Mom didn't have class, I caught a ride with Dad. Oddly enough, it was on these rides with my father that I got what I needed to get through my first heartache. His words gave me the strength to walk away and the courage to try again.

In one of our last car-trip counselling sessions, Dad told me it takes two people communicating, and sometimes communication is hard. Something I've discovered is that when you speak from the heart, often the words that are released are mirrors of what we are neglecting in our own life.

Chapter 7

MY FATHER

*My father was a broken man, doing the best he could
with what he had been taught during his short life.*

In 1954, my dad was the fifth of eight children born in a span of thirteen years. Grandpa had various jobs over his lifetime, including the family homestead, school bus driver, and a stint in the military. He finally settled down and took over the store and post office in Robsart in the mid-'70s.

Grandma's mental health steadily declined with each additional child she had. I heard stories that when she was a young lady, she suffered heat stroke and never was the same. After her second-to-last child, she was institutionalized for a little while. Upon coming home, she found herself pregnant again. This time, she never came home after having the baby. They diagnosed her with schizophrenia.

In those days, it was common practice that women had lots of kids and often raised them on their own because the men were out in the field. Grandma was young and possibly mentally disabled. Add the compounding stress of eight kids in such a short time, and she was exhausted! Postpartum depression was not a recognized or diagnosed in the '50s, and she was subjected to pills and electro-shock therapy as part of her doctor-recommended treatment.

Unfortunately, Dad had very few memories of his mom growing up. Which is why I suspect he and my mom tried to develop a relationship with her when we move to Saskatchewan. While she was hard to understand, largely due to her resistance to wearing her teeth, I believe she was a lovely, lost, beautiful, and funny lady. More recently, she has returned to my life energetically and become a source of guidance.

The eight kids were spread around the area farms. Grandpa did his best to keep who he could. My older aunts spent a lot of time with their dad. Grandpa tried to get them all together when he could, especially holidays. Dad was the middle of three boys and was quite young, maybe four years old, when his mom never came home again. The three boys were regularly passed around the community, sometimes settling with a family for months or years at a time.

My youngest aunt went home with Grandpa's older brother and his partner, June. They raised my Aunt Bee for the majority of her youth. She would later come to live with my dad and mom in her teens to complete high school. My parents made her my godmother—a fitting title, as she would be an active participant through my entire life for guidance.

With few boundaries and little regular family love and support, Dad fell into crowds that were mostly older kids. He smoked and drank while still a child. By grade nine, he had dropped out of school, and around age sixteen, he started doing manual labour. He had a great work ethic and made good money. He lived the good life of working and partying. Around age eighteen, he crossed paths with my mom at a truck-stop restaurant where she was working.

The more you know about the past, the better prepared you are for the future.—Theodore Roosevelt (1858-1919)

I never saw Dad drink from the time he was charged until my sister began to sneak and hide her alcohol in the vehicles on the property. It had to have been close to five years before I discovered Dad was drinking again. I remember coming home from university for visits and Dad's truck would be parked at Rusty's Bar. Of course I stopped and found him hunched over the VLT just dropping rolls of loonies into the machine. I remember thinking to myself, *At least he's not drinking.* I never knew the extent of his gambling addiction until his life had ended.

I graduated in 1997 and left home months later. The year 2000 was a big year, as my sister Amy had graduated high school and Mom had completed her nursing diploma. For the past couple of years, Mom had been staying with Riley and me during the week and home on weekends to complete her nursing course at the college in Lethbridge.

While she was growing, Dad was regressing. He had been borrowing money to pay for and fuel his addiction to gambling. He also had started drinking again.

All Dad's life, relationship after relationship, he had felt abandoned. Whether it was the stress of changing family dynamics, fear of further change and abandonment, or something else, Dad had never learned to deal with his emotions.

Diseases of the soul are more dangerous than those of the body.—English Proverb

He was finally diagnosed with a form of autoimmune-related arthritis, and his pain restricted his ability to work. The company he worked for accommodated his restrictions, because Dad had known many of them a long time. Despite his disabilities, he still had a great work ethic and was a good employee.

The discomfort continued to grow, and Dad continued to decline emotionally, mentally, and physically. My visits weren't as frequent, because at this time, I was attending university full-time and working two jobs. My occasional visits usually led to drinking and dance parties, like when I was a child.

I remember Riley dancing with my mom. She was so happy, and both were very intoxicated. This wasn't a normal look for Riley, but it was fun to see him getting along with my parents. His parents hadn't been as warm and fuzzy as what I was used too.

Dad eventually lost his job as a result of his drinking. Those who loved Dad thought it was a set up. Was it individuals out to get him? Or the universe once again giving Dad a kick in the ass? The end result was that Dad lost his job and Mom was now the sole breadwinner in the house. Dad was transforming into a very old, broken man right before my eyes.

The finish line was in sight, not just for me but also for my dad. His discomfort had reached new heights, and it was difficult for him to function daily. Doctors kept telling him it was the arthritis; they'd increase his steroids and pain pills and send him back home. But by July 2002, Dad could barely walk, and he'd developed a bump and excessive swelling on his face.

That fall, I got the news no child wants to hear. The doctor had found a mass in Dad's lungs and suspected cancer that had metastasized to his bones. The prognosis wasn't good, but Dad was determined to beat it. He told me he would fight hard and beat the odds. He didn't want to give up and have a cure discovered the day after he died. He was mad at himself for continuing to smoke and stopped the day of his diagnosis in the parking lot of Superstore.

The chemo was hard on him. What was harder was how most of his friends and family avoided seeing him in his weak state. He was abandoned again.

In October, the tests confirmed that the tumour had shrunk. However, the excitement was short-lived; soon after, we discovered the cancer had made its way to his brain. Radiation started right away, and after the first treatment, Dad gave in to the disease. He had just turned 48, and the radiation caused paralysis to the left side of his body.

I quit both jobs, focused as much as I could on school, and made trips down every weekend so we could be together as a family. Christmas 2002 was hard. My parents booked a room at the lodge, which was something we normally did around Christmas. Dad and I escaped to the lounge, and I listened as he told me about his regrets and fears—how much he loved all of us and how he was worried about how Mom would cope once he was gone. He worried about her and the family's ability to be there for each other.

That day, I made a promise to him. I would be the glue that kept the family together. Sometimes, it has turned out, it's had and I have to be very stretchy glue, but I intend to keep my promise.

In February 2003, I was able to spend Dad's final week with him, since I had the week off from university. Dad slept almost all the time at this point, only waking to use the bathroom and take his next dose of pain meds. Amy and I had tried to convince him to try marijuana, but Dad wouldn't budge despite the inability to conquer his pain. It was illegal, and we all suspect he didn't want to set another bad example for his daughters.

The morning after I left, I got a phone call from Mom that Dad had taken a turn for the worse, and it was time to come back and say our goodbyes. We rushed back and spent the entire day as a family by his side. We told stories of the lessons we learned and the moments we felt his protection and pride. Right before I left for the night, I let him know what an amazing dad he was, and that I knew he'd stick around and be a great guardian angel.

I left the hospital and went back to the acreage, where I lay in his ugly recliner and cried for hours. Then the pain stopped! It was like a warm blanket or a hug wrapped around me. I got up, wiped my tears, and wandered into the kitchen. The clock on the microwave said 1:17.

About twenty minutes later, my mom called to let me know Dad had passed away at 1:15. His pain was gone. I said I know, he stopped and gave me a hug on the way out.

My dad's body was laid to rest at the end of the week. But his soul continues to guide me and others in achieving our life purposes.

Do Not Stand by My Grave and Weep

Do not stand at my grave and weep
I am not there. I do not sleep.
I am a thousand winds that blow.
I am the diamond glints on snow
I am the sunlight on ripened grain.
I am the gentle autumn rain.
As you awake with morning's hush
I am the swift, up-lifting rush
Of quiet birds in circled flight.
I am the day transcending night.
Do not stand, by at my grave and cry;
I am not there. I did not die.

—Mary Elizabeth Frye

Chapter 8

SPREADING MY
INDIGO WINGS

*Sometimes you need to take a leap. To see how far
you can fly, and where you need to land.*

Growing up, I didn't want kids. I had one pregnancy scare in my teens. While some girls share this fear with their boyfriend at the time to keep him, I did it because I thought my life was over. My plan to graduate high school, hop on a plane the next day, and take off to backpack across Europe was threatened. If I ran out of money, the plan was to call my parents and ask for help to get back home.

I worked hard and saved as much as I could. My first job was at the dry cleaners when I was 15. Six months later, an older girl who worked there encouraged me to ask for a raise. She had informed me I wasn't even making minimum wage. I hated the job and never asked for a raise; instead, I found another job working in a photo development lab. It was a perfect fit and I stayed there until I graduated.

It wasn't Europe that I left to explore. While I often act spontaneously, I do proceed with caution. With nobody to travel with, I opted for a closer adventure. Since my girlfriends decided to start their education and I had no partner in crime to go on an adventure with, I moved to a place I had only been to maybe once before: Lethbridge.

I never gave up on my European dream. Didn't then, and won't now. More then twenty-five years later, and despite travel restrictions for being unvaccinated, I will get there. I just haven't reached that part of my journey. I have a few more things to experience before I get there.

I married the man I moved to Lethbridge with, and we have remained together—twenty-five years as of June 2022. We married because that is what society and family pressure directed us toward. It's all part of the journey! First comes love (1997), then marriage (2004), then completing a degree (2004) to help pay for the house to fill with 2.5 children. At which time, I would be expected to leaving an excellent paying job (2009) to raise the children almost completely alone while the male of the house continues to make the money and purchase what he feels is needed.

I've never been one for following what is expected. I did fall into this prehistoric cycle and suppressed my authentic self for a long stretch of time. One day I woke up and realized this wasn't our life we were living, and decided it was time to change. I remember picking up my phone after a long day of fighting with kids and my husband. Exhausted! Up with the sun and fighting to get my three sons down for the night. It didn't matter how hard I worked, I felt undervalued as a mother. I messaged three words to my mom: "I am sorry."

Boys, or males in general, are fascinating creatures. I mentioned that I was one of five daughters and now a mother of three boys in four years. I love how each one is unique, with different interests, abilities, goals, and personalities. My first, Nathan, slept through the night from day one. I had to wake him every three hours to feed him. Once the jaundice cleared up, I just let him sleep. He was so happy, and I was so rested.

I knew I wasn't going to be done at two. My husband argued you should not have more kids than hands. Which is a fair statement, because he wasn't a hands-on daddy.

I remember the day driving down Dunmore Road, suggesting another baby, and *boom*, I was pregnant. Sean was born only eighteen months after Nathan and was the exact opposite. Once I learned about astrology, I discovered they *are* actually opposites. Nathan is an Aries, Sean is a Libra.

Sean never slept unless I slept with him. He used me as a soother. He was a lot smaller than Nathan, and unlike the rest I got when Nathan was a baby, Sean left me exhausted, largely because he never stopped crying unless I held or wore him in a wrap. By the time Sean was five months, in January 2010, I was extremely unhappy, and I cried alongside Sean on a daily basis.

I loved my babies, but when you spend more time locking them in their cribs because you have the urge to shake them, it's time to get help. Either Sean was broken or I was. The doctor referred me to a psychologist who said I was bipolar and wanted to medicate me. At this point, I was thinking of my grandma who was diagnosed with schizophrenia. I didn't know it then, but it was Grandma showing me the similarities.

I called my mom, horrified with my diagnosis. At this point, my mom had already been working on the psych floor of a hospital for many years. She calmly said, "Crystal, you aren't bipolar. You just had two babies in a very short time frame, one of them hasn't stopped crying, and it is winter. This time of year you always have struggled through. You need to start exercising again and spending time on you."

She was 100 per cent right! Instead of medicating, I went with a friend who had asked me to join her and her co-workers to a new hot yoga studio that had recently opened. We ended up signing up for twice a week, then picked up a third. I refocused my energy after an inaccurate diagnosis, when he should have seen it for what it was, postpartum depression.

I also made the decision to surrender my career as a city planner to raise the boys. The depression lifted, and I shed so much weight, bringing my confidence up. Best part was my Sean stopped crying.

Before learning that their astrology charts put them on opposite sides of the sky-map, I said that my sons were as similar as black and white. Nathan was huge when he was born, slept all the time, and loved to make people smile. As he got older, we discovered he loved to perform and was a big people pleaser. Sean was a little spitfire, too impatient to wait to be delivered by a doctor. He was crawling by five months and running by nine months. He potty-trained himself by eighteen months, small and mighty. Libra to his core! He is judge, jury, and executioner to all matters of his life. There is no telling this boy what to do.

Nathan studied and figured out how things worked before he preformed to perfection. Sean learned best through experience—trial and error. Nathan loved the car bench; Sean was my little naked chef. Both boys packed a doll around at their grandmas; however, my third son, Kade, was repulsed by the baby.

Kade's personality was as if you took a copy of both Nathan and Sean and crammed it into one package. Then, because there was so much personality, the powers that be felt they needed Kade to be unmovable. I don't think there is a more stubborn creature that walks this planet. I never knew what personality I was going to pull out of the crib at the start of the day with that one.

With Kade becoming a new mom, I had new tools to cope. I learned that I had to take care of myself first and foremost, because a happy mom made the house and kids more balanced. Yoga was my saving grace; however, it was just the start. It taught me that I am stronger than I thought I was, and every time the journey gets rough, I land myself back on my mat to ground and refocus.

So many, including me, start yoga with the expectation that there is a right and a wrong way to do it. Yoga is for everybody, and it's not fitness. It is a personal journey to reignite the love you had before judgment was planted, making you feel inadequate.

My first two pregnancies were high risk, and I ended up on bed rest for the third trimester. But despite the assault on my mental, emotional, and physical body, I wanted one more. I also decided to set up a savings account and went to work making and selling baby items at the farmers markets.

I had lost a bunch of weight after Sean, and I still had a dough belly I was ashamed of. At five foot four inches, an inch shorter than my mom, the only way I could house a growing baby with my frame was out. That would, and did, result in a completely separated diastasis recti, plus a lot of extra stretchmarks and skin.

While I continued to save, lose weight, and plan for another baby, there was a deadline to convince my husband to have one more. He'd booked a vasectomy for September 2010. I thought June 2010, would give me another April baby, making Sean and Baby Three two and a half years apart. As the date drew closer, I grieved the loss of the child I would never have.

But the universe knew we needed another angel to help with our life lessons. One thing led to another, and a third boy was born in May 2011. Kade was my final baby. My heart was full.

Nothing prepared me for the emotional responsibility of becoming a parent. From that moment of seeing the second pink line, my life forever changed. The physical string was cut at birth. However, I continue to feel their joys and sorrows. I can read their emotions, just as they can read mine.

The boys were busy, but they got along great. I returned to yoga around eight weeks post-Kade, and the time flew by the next few years. My body felt strong, and my boys made me very tired but also very happy.

In April 2013, I would spend over six hours in surgery and in excess of $10,000 as countless internal stitches were put into place. On the surface, I had pieced my physical body back together. But internally, I continued to fester. The surgery had helped to remove the marks of motherhood; however, the scar ironically held together my unraveling unhappiness. While I had surrendered my body, my career, my freedom, I felt so alone.

I began to resent my husband's lack of participation. Within twenty-four hours of arriving home post-surgery to make my body more desirable for him, I was left home alone with our three boys between the ages of six and not quite two. Tubes were coming out of me, and a drainage bag was still attached. I was left alone to swallow my frustrations.

The resentment grew for about a year, and on March 6, 2014, days before my thirty-fourth birthday, my body began to scream out that it had had enough. This was another journey where I chose the path against doctor recommendations.

It started as a simple kidney stone and ended in the failure of a kidney and its removal. The local doctor's best guess was genetic kidney disease—a fair assumption, as this was one of the leading factors that shortened my grandmother Josie's life. She had lost both kidneys and was on dialysis for years prior to heart failure.

Doctors denied my pain, stating that a non-functioning kidney does not cause pain. But to me, the pain was real. My body was screaming. The pain was so real, there were days when I couldn't get out of bed.

I continued to make and sell at the farmers market and run kids around. Yoga took the back burner due to headaches and side-effects from the medication. I tried to focus on a holiday I was saving for: Disneyland.

After almost a year from the start of my kidney problems, I finally got a referral to a surgeon in Calgary. February 2015 was my consult, and as luck would have it, there was a cancelation just two months away. I would get the surgery shortly after we got back from Disneyland.

Disneyland is advertised as the happiest place on earth, a place where dreams can come true. For me, this was were I started to wake up and realize my prince wasn't very charming.

We spent nine days in California. I did all the planning and saved the money. It was important to plan for the rainy season, because Riley doesn't like sun or heat. Too bad Mother Nature didn't get the memo. That year, California was hit with a heat wave, and Riley was not a happy person to be around.

We tried to get a reprieve from the heat, but hiding out in the hotel with three boys isn't an option. I spent a good chunk of my time poolside alone with the boys soaking up the sun. There is definitely a perk to have your kids close together; they can be good at keeping each other entertained.

I watched the boys and tried to figure out how I could have made the holiday better for Riley. I remember crying by the pool, and one of the boys giving me a hug, so I got up and got in the pool. I was in a place where dreams come true. I was at Disneyland, the place my parents promised to take us to, and instead I made it happen and had my mom fly out too join us for a couple of days. This was all my doing, and Riley was making me feel like the holiday was horrible. Is this really who I wanted to spend the rest of my life with?

When the holiday was over, it was back to reality and my surgery. Riley talked a lot about the holiday. But it was more about how much it cost him and little about what we actually did and saw. At first, it bugged me how much he took credit for the expense. I worked hard, saved every penny I could gather, and he groaned about how much it cost. He covered the extras, like the food we bought at the grocery store and some of the meals out—a drop in the bucket compared to my contributions.

He complained, and the cost he paid seemed to keep going up. We didn't do another holiday until 2017. It would be just the two of us, and it went even more disastrously than this one.

I had my surgery on April 24, and six weeks later, the biopsy showed that the kidney had chronically abscessed cysts, and it was good that it had been removed. Had a cyst ruptured, my body would have gone septic within hours. This explained why the pain would flare up, and after each flare-up the pain would temporarily disappear after a course of antibiotics.

This wasn't the first time the doctor argued with me about a course of treatment. This time, however, the stakes of the outcome were a matter of life and death. I chose correctly.

It was this event that led me to question every recommendation a health professional would make. Yes, they went to school for a long time, spent thousands of dollars on their education and endless hours working with people, but after only a few years of practicing yoga, I knew I knew my body better then anyone ever could.

Kintsugi or *kintsukuroi* is a method of repairing ceramics with lacquer and gold. It leaves a gold seam where the cracks were. It is believed to give the piece a new and more refined aspect. I see my scars as trophies that celebrate the challenges I have overcome.

Healing doesn't happen overnight. We are shown the lesson and see how it could make a change in our life. But change is scary, and I had to be willing to face my fears in order to make the necessary change happen. This came in the way of a pregnancy scare. Turned out my B12 was so low, my periods had stopped. I didn't realize my food sensitivities, to gluten and dairy, were also my body letting me know I needed change. I tested for allergies, but results were negative.

My body hurt all the time. My kidney levels were better then fine; however, with every ache and pain suffered, my family doctor finally just blamed it on having one kidney. Eventually, she recommended I start water pills.

It was when she made this recommendation that I remembered those visits with my Grandma Josie. In her kitchen, she had a small round table that was covered with pills. When we sat down, she would sweep a hand over the table, moving all her pills to one side. The clearing gave us a space to sit and have a sandwich and gingersnap cookies. I took the prescription note and left. I never took the prescription in.

I had been receiving a B12 injection every three weeks, which I figured out how to self-administer. I didn't think it was a big deal, but it confused me, because I did eat pretty healthy. My grandma Josie was a big lady with a healthy German appetite. So I wanted to curb my curves and be conscious about food choices and staying active. Easier said than done, because I was a comfort eater.

My plan was to find what foods I needed so that I could stop the injections. What I learned was that my problem wasn't my food choices. There was something creating inflammation in my intestines, preventing the B12, which is in meat sources, from being absorbed.

Around this time, a local yoga studio was offering yoga teacher training. It took some convincing, but Riley fronted me the money. I learned over the years that if I really wanted something, I needed to sell it to Riley as an investment. As a certified yoga teacher, I wouldn't be working a lot, which meant I still had time to be a full-time wife, mother, cook, house cleaner …

To me, this wasn't an investment in our house. This was me giving permission to myself to be selfish and, yes, a little narcissistic manipulating Riley to get what I wanted. I wanted this teacher training for *me*. I needed to learn more about how yoga was helping me and take my practice to the next level. The practice of yoga had helped me, but I never knew why.

It was my third attempt to register for a two-hundred-hour yoga teacher training program. The first two were through a Baptiste or affiliate school. I love Baptiste power yoga; I consider it my roots, and it always brings me back when I feel stuck. However, in my previous registrations, there weren't enough students, so the classes were cancelled.

The third time I registered for 200YTT, it was hosted by two local female yoga teachers with very different teaching styles. The owner of the studio was strong and very masculine in her theory. She helped me find the strength to show my authentic self. The other teacher was very intuitive and feminine in her style, forcing us students to address old wounds and heal our emotional self.

I realized I held a lot of resentment buried inside me, as well as a default of being comfortable in the discomfort of being abandoned. This program was exactly what I needed. It was scary, and not pretty in any way. Most weekends I spent crying, physically and emotionally exhausted when it was done. I found my voice, remembered who I was, and learned how to use this rediscovered knowledge to speak my truth: "I am adventurous!"

The Five Reiki Principles

Just for today, I will not be angry.
Just for today, I will not worry.
Just for today, I will be grateful.
Just for today,
I will do my work honestly.
Just for today, I will be kind
to every living thing.
—Dr. Mikao Usui

First, you learn to love yourself. Then you feel it spill out, and it becomes possible to harvest this excess to help heal others. By the third weekend of YTT, I felt like I was crying all the time. This is when I was introduced to Reiki.

It blows my mind that in history, when a man did this, he was recognized as a god, a divine immortal being. If a woman claimed to use this same gift to heal, she was called a witch. History is full of the torture, burning, and drowning of mostly women who had the gift to heal. Bills, legislation, and books were commissioned by high-ranking men attempting to explain the unexplainable, creating fear and division.

In my classes, I describe Yang (masculine) energy as structure, logic, reason, and wisdom from the mind. Yin (feminine) energy is irrational, illogical, unexplainable, undefined knowledge from the heart and soul. Our exterior differences in gender should not create division at the soul level. We have and should use both. We need to drop our labels, remove judgment, and just love each person for their unique combination of yang and yin energy.

Love is patient, love is kind. It does not envy, it does not boast, it is not proud. It does not dishonour others, it is not self-seeking, it is not easily angered, it keeps no record of wrongs. Love does not delight in evil but rejoices with the truth. It always protects, always trusts, always hopes, always perseveres. Love never fails. But where there are prophecies, they will cease; where there are tongues, they will be stilled; where there is knowledge, it will pass away.—1 Corinthians 13:4-8 NIV

Chapter 9

RILEY'S RED FLAGS

When we enter a relationship we create a character for our new partner to play a part in our story. When you are only eighteen, you don't realize that that character you fell in love with comes with a story of his own. Within his story you will be his co-star, and play the part he assigns to you in his story. I gave up my story to be in his.

To this day, I have no clue why I called him the next day. Since turning 18 in March of 1997, I was loving the nightclub scene. I got in trouble a time or two for being a tease, but I was pretty conservative for the most part and was no bar bunny. I loved to dance and welcomed the attention, which often led to free drinks, but I rarely got drunk. There was always a designated driver who took responsibility for our group while at the bar, events around town, or during grad activities.

June 13 was the chem-free party that my friends and I attended. However, we all decided to hit a local club the next evening. I struck up a deal with one of my girlfriends' dads to enable her to come to my place, where there was no curfew.

On June 14, after sleeping most of the day away, we all got dressed up and headed out to Essie's Nightclub, the hot spot at the time. The night was ours, and all I had to do to have my girlfriend stay over was crawl out of bed and be at church before lunch the next day.

What I anticipated and what I showed up for was not what I expected. This was no Catholic service with benches, hymns, and choir songs. This was the loudest group of hand-clapping, dancing, belting-out-songs-at-the-top-of-their-lungs gospel church music I had thought only existed in movies. I had made a deal with the devil! I had attended a Catholic service from time to time with an old boyfriend hung over; that was do-able. This … I had to sit down, because I didn't know if I was going to puke or pass out. I survived, and when it was over, I headed back to her place, where I called him—Riley.

It was normal for me to collect numbers. It was also normal for me to give out fake numbers. But for some odd reason, I got this guy's number and called him the next day. I knew his name from high school. He was a grade ahead of me and honestly kind of a jerk. I had dated a friend of his years before and had had a major crush on a friend of his until recently.

I think about that night. He was wearing a white Mondetta sweater. I was dressed in white jeans and a tank top. Both of us were glowing under the black lights. I have no doubt that our souls were contracted to get together to teach each other life lessons. There was obviously something greater at work behind the scenes for me to call this guy after a drunk bar-floor make-out session. Something had to be in order for us to survive three kids and twenty-five years of ups and downs. It hasn't been easy and we've both made mistakes, but we've used them to learn, and grow.

If you live to be a hundred, I hope I live to be a hundred minus one day, so that I never have to live a day without you.—Winnie the Pooh

A few of my boys are just entering the dating age. The girls they have brought home are always awkward and quiet, probably much like I was. I never had much luck with moms. They always made me feel like I wasn't good enough for their son. That's something I don't want my sons' girlfriends to experience from me.

The longest relationship I had prior to my husband was the boyfriend who broke my heart. It lasted on and off for about eighteen months. The story I was told was his mom took off to join the Jehovah's Witnesses, abandoning her three boys and husband. He had some abandonment issues and trust issues when it came to females.

The oddest breakup was when I dumped a guy I was suppose to take to grad. We were only together for five months. The whole time we talked about grad and planned our outfits to match. Two weeks before, I found out his mom was making him take his older sister, and he was going stag. I dumped him and took one of my friend's brothers with the extra ticket I'd bought.

Becoming a boy mom has been challenging. I used to tell my boys, "Stay away from girls; they don't know what they want. Wait for a woman. They know what they need." Well, karma, thanks for another lesson: a son who skips the gangling preteen years and looks 16 at 13. I had to give my head a shake as my baby told me about all the phone numbers he was given at the local pool, by much older girls. Funny, karma, really funny!

I got lucky with Nathan's first official girlfriend, who was a good gateway to having a daughter-in-law. She was very chatty and tried to spark conversations with everyone in our family. We learned about each other's interests and would team up to tease Nathan.

Having three boys, my hope is that their partners can be the daughters I never had, even if it means my heart gets broken a few times if they aren't meant to be "the one." Yes, sometimes they will disappoint me, just like my sons can. They are kids trying to figure life out.

Hell, I'm still trying to figure it out. But I do know that after twenty-five years, it breaks my heart when my mother-in-law judges Riley or my choices, so why would I repeat her hurtful pattern?

Two amazing women can love the same incredible man in completely different ways. One is his wife, the other is his mother.—Unknown

There is a different bond between mothers and their sons. I've witnessed this with my husband as well as with my boys. Through my courses, I've learned this is a healthy masculine energy. What's not healthy is when mothers see this as a competition, or that they are being replaced.

I can't speak for my mother-in-law, but this is how she has made me feel since the beginning. This unfortunately has placed her son in an unfair position between the two women he loves—something I will not do with my boys and their potential or future partners. If I do, I want them to be honest and put me back in line.

Riley and I grew up figuratively on opposite sides of the tracks. While my parents had many do-overs and little to show for their time on earth, Riley's family lived in a big house on a park-sized lot and drove vehicles with matching fenders. I had worked since I was 15 to provide myself with the extras, including the shampoo of my choosing and tampons instead of the phonebook-sized discount pads my parents bought. Riley worked, but it was to put gas in the car his parents bought him. So when Riley quit his job, racked up speeding tickets, and needed gas money, his mother gave it to him, but restricted him from picking me up.

He didn't like the rules, so he got a job at Sears. Problem solved … for a while. Sears gave him some time, but with fall approaching and Riley not wanting to go to college, it was time for a *real* job. Riley had moved out once before but moved back home. His parents decided it was time to grow up, and he needed a career.

With the help of his dad and some family connections, he got a job interview in Lethbridge with Canadian Pacific Railway. With the exception of a volleyball tournament, I'd never gone to Lethbridge. So it was fun to be swept away for a romantic getaway. I didn't see much of the city beyond the hotel.

Summer was flying by, and despite my girlfriends bailing on

our European adventure, I continued to work and save. I planned to take a year off. I was hoping maybe they would want to go on their next summer break, not realizing the school debt they were building.

My parents had told me I could stay home, but I would have to pay rent. They intended to save it for me to help with college when I was ready. I didn't know if college was in my future. I hated school, and so many adults I looked up to had ingrained in my brain, for as long as I could remember, that I wasn't smart enough. I knew I was. I had Rutherford scholarships to prove it for the semesters I actually tried. But school bored me, and I chose not to apply myself.

I wasn't going to school, wasn't staying home, so I needed to find a roommate. As summer came to a close, Riley found out he got the job in Lethbridge and had to move there at the beginning of October. We had only been together for a couple of months, and when he showed up to tell me, I thought we would either have to do long-distance or break up. I tried to beat him to the punch and stormed off before he could break my heart. It was cute how he chased me down, threw me over his shoulder, and carried me back to my room. He insisted we were going out to celebrate, and instead of a breakup, he asked me to move with him. I said yes!

You get more from life when you take each
opportunity and treat it like a new adventure.

Building up to the move was exciting and scary. The month before, we started nesting. I had a double bed with matching dresser set, and we purchased a second-hand love seat which we shampooed. Our family didn't feel complete with just Gizmoe, so we adopted a second cat and named her Gabby.

On October 2, we loaded everything up—the majority of the U-Haul was filled with black garbage bags full of Riley's name-brand clothes—and set off on our adventure. I cried the whole way there. Riley couldn't get me to stop, so he ended up calling my mom.

It was probably her telling me that I could come home that stopped the tears.

His parents came up the following day to take us grocery shopping. At this point, Riley was still paying down debt to his parents. So in order for his parents to be on board with me coming with, they made sure I paid my share of everything.

Riley's mom took us shopping. I paid half, and she added his half to the tab she had. In those days, Riley's checks came on a piece of paper, so he was expected to pretty much sign the back and give it to his mom. He did, except for the Nintendo 63 he bought so we had some kind of entertainment. She wasn't impressed but continued to give him an allowance.

We ate what she approved. By the end of October, my account was nearing zero and I had put on a lot of weight. It hurt how Riley's family pointed out how big I was getting, like I didn't see the stretchmarks appearing or that the only thing that still fit were pyjama pants and sweats. I really didn't need them to tell me.

Depression, my old friend, was showing its ugly face. I needed a purpose, and I needed money. So Riley's mom helped me get a job with the franchise she worked at. I hated it, but it was income and only seasonal, so I was done around Christmas. This job bridged the gap between going broke and having to go home with my tail between my legs, which I was grateful for. I could continue to pay my half and feel worthy staying with Riley.

I also discovered that Europe wasn't in my immediate future, so I needed to return to school and make some real money. When the job had come to an end, I found one working retail in the mall. Riley decided after only a few paychecks to go to the bank and take out a small loan to pay his mom off. He claimed our independence, and it was great.

We decided to find another rental and moved in February 1998. This one was a little bit more money but located in Lethbridge, not Coalhurst. Extra perk, it had a cute fireplace, which at the time we thought was so romantic.

We worked out our own agreement for splitting expenses. He paid the rent; I bought the groceries. I continued to work my retail job and also enrolled at the local high school to upgrade my English so I could attend university. We were growing up and planning a future together. Within couple of weeks, I discovered the upgrading wasn't necessary, and I was accepted into the University of Lethbridge. My decision to get an education and better our future didn't seem to get as much approval from his mother.

It was about a year since we had started living together. Neither of us had anything of value, aside from a Nintendo 64, but his mom felt it was necessary to have a common-law agreement drawn up. His parents paid all legal fees, and all we had to do was sign. I understand they wanted to protect their child, but at this time, there had never been any reason to think I would leave. We still lived in a basement suite. Riley had done what every new railroader does and bought himself a brand-new sports car, so he was swimming in debt. There was no money to protect. The lawyer they paid did his job and advised me not to sign.

Riley wasn't bothered by me not signing the agreement. He actually followed my lead and didn't even meet with his lawyer. I don't think my mother-in-law is an evil or spiteful women. I've learned over the years that some people are addicted to control. When their life story isn't playing out the way they want it to, they can get really creative in their attempt to regain control of the events and people around them. It's taken me a long time to realize that the majority of Riley's family doesn't even realize that this is one of the patterns that is preventing them from truly enjoying life.

Since I was going to university and the rail station was just out the west side of Lethbridge, in Coalhurst, Riley's mom decided she was going to buy a house for us to rent from her. In theory, it sounded like a great plan. We had to pay rent, so why not keep the money in the family? A house was picked, and with the crazy rental prices on the West Side, there was room to rent the basement to a couple of other students.

We weren't opposed to roommates. Over the years, we ended up with many roommates. However, I didn't remember Riley's mom had picked our two female roommates who had her approval. I had actually forgotten about these two girls until I was sharing the clarity I was getting from this writing this book.

We often joked about it, which is probably a bit of a coping strategy for me, to think that in Riley's mom's eyes nobody would have been good enough for him. But last night, before I could judge the response that escaped my lips, I commented, "Except for Tina Sour."

Riley laughed and said, "Remember when Mom wanted to buy a house and have Tina and Natalie move in with us?"

Seriously! Did I black that out? I totally remembered once he said it. Once again evidence in my mind that this other woman in my husband's life did not think I was good enough. For years, every time she would get involved in our life, I'd be triggered. I would react like a crazy lady to get "us" back on track.

His parents bought a new white vehicle, so both Riley's sister and Riley bought a new white vehicle. Riley maybe had the car a year before he showed me a truck he really liked, so he traded the car in. I tried to keep the peace through holidays, trips, a wedding, moving back to Medicine Hat, grandbabies for the next sixteen years. I avoided putting Riley in the middle, but I feel that at some point, I was alone in the fight for us to keep our independence from his family. I started to see that Riley was becoming growingly more concerned with societal and family expectations. And with his concern, he became controlling.

I've learned that when you try to control everything,
you enjoy nothing.—Unknown

There are helicopter parents who want to keep their child safe. I think most moms, especially the first time around, wish they could bubble-wrap their babies as they go explore the world. Having three boys has taught me that in order to keep my sanity, I had to see if they bounced when they fell. Riley, while an amazing dad, still has the old mindset that when a parent barks, kids need to listen and follow instructions immediately.

I started to see the controlling aspects of Riley's personality and how it affected our boys. I caught myself one day informing Riley that if he didn't learn to give the boys some freedom and experience life with natural consequences, he would end up a grumpy, lonely old man like his dad. Nathan, when he was younger, would cower, then chase Riley around seeking approval. Sean barked back, and for a long time, I would just leave. It was like a war had erupted, and nobody listened to Switzerland. I would return and have to pick up the pieces of the two of them when I got home.

Kade was similar to Nathan in his younger years. He would duck in his room for cover, in tears because he didn't feel heard. I attempted to teach all four of the men, big and small, that these patterns were not healthy. COVID lockdowns put a spotlight on the problem. Within only a few months, it became increasingly noticeable the difference in the home environment when Riley was away and when he would be home for a couple of days. Riley has released some of his controlling tendencies, but with growing tension between us, he often resorts to old habits.

There are always red flags when starting a relationship. We all have baggage from the experiences we have had in life. When you see these flags, it's important to ask yourself, *Is this something I can live with or grow from?* Relationships require compromise, and this is resolved through conversation (communication). Baggage or trauma should not be something the other person is required to tippy-toe around. Nobody can walk on eggshells for an extended period of time and remain happy and healthy.

I knew after a year that Riley's mom was a lot to put up with. But I wasn't living with and, later, marrying her. For many years, I felt I was heard by Riley. He did step in and make me feel supported.

However, the abuse continued, and eventually Riley wasn't as involved in the repair. There would be a situation, I would be hurt, and Riley would step in, first by repairing through conversations, then with a gift to make me feel better. The conversations quit happening, the wrongdoings just got swept way, and life would go on. Nobody ever apologized; nobody ever admitted mistakes or errors except me.

The reason recently given after a difference of opinion was that they don't like conflict. Correct: they don't like conflict *if they are in the wrong*. I enabled Riley to continue to appease his parents' choice not to change. Each time his mother insulted me, I just took it, until one summer day in 2017 when it got to be just too much.

Enabling is helping, assisting, supporting, or bailing someone out so they can avoid the natural (and perhaps unpleasant) consequences of their actions. I did it to control fear and guilt but called it love. Enabling had to stop when I noticed my pain and the cyclic insanity resulting from my attempt to protect.

Chapter 10

IN-LAWS

Dear Mother-in-Law: Never tell me how to handle my children. I'm living with one of yours and he needs a lot of improvement. Sincerely, Your Daughter-in-Law—Unknown

"Then let them call social services. They will see that I am a good mom. My boys are loud, happy, and safe."

Two days later, me standing up for myself led to a hurricane of conflict. Accusations were made based on presumptions and lack of communication. We left the cabin within minutes after only being there for a few days. It wasn't the first time our ten-hour drive resulted in a hasty exit. It *was* the first time my kids had to see Mom losing her shit toward Grandma.

I swore I would never return, and I haven't. I left that place of judgment and fake wealth, and I have no intention of going back. While I was unable to walk away from a relationship with this woman, I created boundaries in an attempt to maintain my marriage.

Boundaries work great provided there are no leaks in the metaphoric wall. I have seen how my mom's fractured relationship with her in-laws prevented my dad and his siblings from connecting.

It put Dad in the middle. I didn't want this for Riley. So I attempted to keep her updated with the kids' accomplishments and activities, phone calls, and occasionally going over. I knew that I needed relationship boundaries, and I wanted to give my children the option to decide for themselves if they wanted a relationship with these people.

I had, until COVID mandates, been able to sit at a table, eat a supper, or park my butt on a bench in the backyard, as the "family" talks. I do not engage, despite the occasional button-pushing into my beliefs or business practices. This judgment and criticism I feel comes from a lack of interest and information, ignorance, and fear. I don't own this judgment and have successfully chosen to live without their energy influencing my life.

> *You can lead a horse to water, but you can't*
> *make it drink.—English Proverb*

I attempted to verbally explain my boundaries to Riley. It wasn't until the pandemic that Riley realized the reason for my boundaries. It became apparent that I did not agree with anything mainstream pushed out, while Riley's parents drank the media's Kool-Aid. I'd show up at a rally, or in a news article, and they would express their concern and disgust to Riley over my involvement. Multiple times, they told him it would be easier if Crystal just did as she was told. Riley stood by me, often pointing out the obvious: "You really don't know her, do you?"

The pandemic continued; weeks turned to months and then years. So many rules, changing without medical evidence to support the decisions. Governments around the world kept finding medical "professionals" to give their opinion, versus showing real data supporting their decisions.

Riley's family became embarrassed by my speaking out and would call Riley, speechless due to their friends who felt sorry that they had a daughter-in-law like me. In my defence, I was proud that my son made the paper for his stand and participation in the walkout responding to the Freedom Convoy. While I was fighting the battle for the mental health of my kids, Riley was frequently being bombarded with political propaganda by his family and friends.

Conversations weren't ever about asking how the boys and I were doing. I had to close my business and still pay rent. I had three kids who had to stay home and homeschool. "Stay home" protected the most vulnerable, they said. There was no compassion toward others. There was only guilt and complaints about all the health problems people had, and it was everyone's responsibility to control the germs that could kill.

Everyone became vulnerable, and the only cure that would open up the world was vaccinations. Each incentive the government announced had me on my toes. I was always looking for ways for our family to avoid this medical treatment until they could show me the data on its safety.

I never gave Riley an ultimatum. He never asked, but the truth is, this untested medical procedure scared me. Riley chose to listen to his parents' instructions versus asking me questions to understand my fears. I know things happened the way they were supposed to. Riley's decision to follow the pressure of friends and family is part of his journey, but unfortunately, it has created a rift once again in our marriage.

Christmas 2021 was a nightmare. Personal beliefs, individual fears, and nearly two years of government encouraging division between friends and family made gatherings through our darkest months impossible. Travel bans and social restrictions for the unvaccinated left many people power-hungry to push their own agendas and beliefs on others. Even our country's leader, Mr. Trudeau, was throwing divisive terms like *racist* and *misogynistic* at people who simply didn't want to take the COVID vaccination.

Personally, I don't care what a person's beliefs are, my door is always open, especially through the Christmas season. Over the last few years, I had spent too much time watching people's mental health slip from lack of social interaction. So I decided to open my home to everyone.

My in-laws were among the people who cancelled Christmas. Not only was I not willing to limit my exposure to other people, I refused to mask my unvaccinated kids and myself in order to do Christmas supper. My lack of conforming led to a text, which I did see firsthand. In it, Riley's mom asked him to bring the kids by their house while I was at work so they could be "together as a family." I'm so grateful Riley saw through the division they were trying to create.

I have never lowered my metaphoric walls. What I need now is for Riley to see just how deep the wounds they cut are and to make the choice to build some walls of his own. I don't expect or even want Riley to cut his family out of his life. They can be lovely humans, and we need family. But sometimes it's better and more healthy to love them from a distance. When we make people uncomfortable through boundary creation, it often forces them to reflect and do some needed change and growth themselves.

I am the only one responsible for making the choices to create my happiness. I cannot control how Riley or his family will behave in the future, but I can create an environment to teach my boys to break this pattern of controlling other people, and that allowing others to dictate happiness does not equal love.

From the outside, twenty-five years looks like a happy home. But behind the drawn curtains and locked doors, there is an opportunity for love to be replaced by repression and resentment.

Part Two
THE PRESENT

Chapter 11

MASTER

Once upon a time, in lands far away, people looked up to their elders. Now you can be a 28-year-old god with a PhD. Your credibility and worth is measured by the name and quality of paper you hang on the wall. The majority of this world's inhabitants want to see a piece of paper, your credentials, as proof that you know what you're talking about.

I have met so many people who have taken up to and including the Master Level training of Reiki, yet they continue to talk about the darkness in others. I've lost count of how many people I've heard from who didn't want to give energy work another chance because some "healer" told them about the evil attached to them, how their energy made the healer physical ill or hurt them. This is not the client's fault; this is what I would refer to as energetic malpractice. This is a twofold healer problem and not the client's.

Usui's original teachings included three levels. The Master program was something added on later. I do have the piece of paper, but I refuse to call myself a Master. I strive to one day, but as of now, I have so much to learn, and I am much too young. Maybe by the time I'm 108, I will have the experience and credentials.

> *What you think, you become. What you feel, you*
> *attract. What you imagine, you create.*—*Buddha*

I've watched as a young man named Jay transformed from a terrified child. Jay had a life of trauma, including sexual abuse and lack of support around his sexuality, beliefs, and interests. Society's assumptions led to the misdiagnosis and mistreatment of Jay's symptoms. Adding to the trauma Jay experienced were the words of another healer who claimed to see a "darkness" around him. The healer claimed to be physically harmed by this darkness, leading Jay to believe that this evil entity would try to harm or kill anyone who tried to help him.

After a few sessions, and me not being harmed, Jay's imagination helped him conclude that I was an angel sent to heal him. What you imagine, you create. I should have been flattered, but the truth is, his thought process and words terrified me.

I looked to see who his family doctor was on the intake form, but of course, he'd left it blank. Was he having some kind of psychotic break? Lucifer was an angel cast from heaven. Would my client connect me to this parable and make the connection that I was evil?

I asked the universe, through prayer, to let this client continue his healing journey, but for our relationship to continue through prayer only. Jay left our sessions with a positive mindset. It lead to a reduction in his depression and anxiety. He increased his energetic frequency, and healed his mental and emotional health on his own, which allowed him to taper off and eventually stop all meds, doctor-prescribed and street. The psychosis stopped.

About six months later, Jay walked into the store. When I saw him in person that day, I realized why we came together. The fear I felt was the fear his previous healers had felt. This fear was not Jay's; it was the reflection of what Jay and I had in common. Jay saw his own greatness. It came to him in the form of a story he understood to be angelic. I see this now because I saw it in Jay that day in the store.

See yourself in the most majestic embodiment possible. Now think bigger! This is only a fraction of your potential. Denial keeps you in the dark.

I still reach out and send Jay love from time to time when he passes my thoughts. While this lesson is completed, the connection between teacher and student is eternal. Jay was a great teacher. The energy you put out is an invitation to attract. The clients who are attracted to me also help me take the next step in my journey.

With the hundreds of clients I've seen, I connect based on mirrors. What I feel is related to my past experiences, healed or denied. If I am uncomfortable, it is a result of something the other person embodies that I am usually repressing in myself. If a healer ever tells you they see "darkness," it is their own darkness that they are not currently shining a light on.

A person isn't just light/dark or good/evil. We are energetic beings, a living spectrum of light and shade. It is not only okay but necessary to sit in our darkness. This is how we get to know, love, and own our whole self. We are complete, and the only way to accept our complete package is to explore our light, darkness, and everything in between.

Without a strong-enough awareness of one's personal energy levels, protection, and grounding, a sudden shift in frequency can leave practitioners unsettled in their own energetic field. As the Master with a piece of paper, so many feel invincible. We forget that every Master is living the human experience, and the first thing any of us wants to do is give reason to a sudden shift in how we feel. We want to live in light and love, but there is always the opportunity for ego to step in, pushing us into a space of fear.

Generation after generation, we have been taught to shift blame. Spoiler alert: whether you consider yourself an average Joe or a mystical being, the darkness witnessed is your own.

Shadow Work is going within the dark recesses of your psyche and finding the shadows that lurk. Find the parts of you that you've repressed or rejected through the years. Find them, feel them, heal them, and let it all go. This is the kind of spiritual work that leads to never ending peace and joy.—Unknown

Chapter 12

LOVE, FEAR, AND THE MIND

To fear love is to fear life, and those who fear life are
already three parts dead.—Bertrand Russell

Love has be scientifically measured to have a much higher frequency than fear. At 528 Hz, it is visible to see healing of an individual at the level of their DNA. Study results vary numerically as to at what frequency cell destruction starts; however, it is conclusive in all studies that emotions like guilt, resentment, anger, and fear result in the death of cellular tissues.

I am open to conversations on entities. The only darkness I've ever experienced in the hundreds of people I've seen is fear. This is why a lot of my focus in life as well as with my guiding is to help my students and clients work through their own fears. It results in the building of their strength and destroying of their darkness. This is often referred to as *shadow work*.

First, one must love oneself; then one will know how to love another. We all seek approval from the outside world. It is human to want to find reason or excuses. Fact or fiction, we don't care, because with the assistance of memory and imagination, the story creates a visual allowing us to connect through our senses. To understand, we must *see*. Physical sight grounds the thoughts we want to believe in as a truth. If we can see something to be a truth, it makes us feel mentally competent (less crazy/nuts).

Sleep, or rest of any kind, is probably the best gift we can give ourselves and our children. Mom used to say, "I hope you have a daughter just like you." I'll admit it, I was, and still can be, a bit of a handful. In a world of restrictions, it's nice to have a place to escape without consequence.

Dreams have helped me get through heartbreaks and cope with grief, and have taken me to places life has stopped me from reaching. Dreams have allowed me to have, be, and do what appears out of reach. I am able to play out scenarios in my dreams before they happen to find an ideal outcome. As well, my dreams have prevented me from making some horrible mistakes. I didn't realize it at the beginning of my journey, but the ability to dream helped me get back to my authentic self, finding that adventurous part of me that I lost.

Ego is a creation of society's programs (seeds) embedded in our minds. Intuition is the creation of the heart and soul when they work in harmony. When we are awake ego, our masculine/logical mind is in control. In sleep intuition, the feminine mind runs the show.

Ego makes decisions based on fear; intuition, on love. While awake, we are faced with situations that we must make a decision about based on reasons defined by a source, such as our beliefs, peers, or society's rules and expectations. Our intuition usually takes a back seat in our daily waking hours. However, from time to time, we experience that gut feeling that something is right or wrong.

Ego bases choices on the level of fear. *Intuition* uses the quality of the feelings produced from the union of heart and soul to explore the choices. Intuition is not a measurable construct, and oftentimes the feeling-based choice is dismissed due to the inability to explain why something is right or wrong.

When we sleep, we visit these circumstances of decision. In an unconscious dream state, without the pressure of bringing a decision into fruition, we see our heart's desire as well as our fears.

However, these are rarely presented in a logical way. My intuition communication is generally not logical. Instead, it's almost like a riddle for me to solve in the form of pictures, words, ideas, and more.

Ego wants reasons and explanations, so often, without logic, ego can talk us out of things. Have you ever been in a situation where you had a great idea and told yourself you needed to sleep on it? Could you? Or did you spend the whole night overthinking, convincing, and not sleeping a wink?

Insomnia is plaguing the world. At the end of my teens through my twenties and most of my thirties, I accepted lack of sleep as normal. But insomnia should not be normalized. As with the physical body, when we ignore the signs of mental discomfort, it leads to disease. Our bodies need sleep so we can dream. Food is digested to nourish our physical bodies, while dreams are an opportunity to digest for our mental and emotional (energetic) bodies.

Discomfort that keeps us awake intensifies into diseases like sleep apnea. Lack of sleep means the body cannot rest and digest. No digestion, no healing. Sure, there are pills, teas, and tinctures that can promote sleep. The most abused form of sleep aid comes as nightcaps or THC, but once again, these are just Band-Aids. The chemicals you are self-treating with are harming your liver and do not fix the underlying problem that is keeping you up at night.

Humans live in a world where we literally need to unplug. We go, go, go, come home, and plug in. Our physical body surrenders, but our minds are still in overdrive. In the future, I plan to explore methods that create a better balance between resting and wakeful states, but for now, unplug, get a book, and read until your eyes feel heavy and you fall asleep. If the mind is busy and the words on the page are just letters, get an audiobook, close your eyes, and create a movie screen with the narrator's words. Books of any form allow an individual a focal point for controlling the mind.

Meditation is not a monk sitting in lotus pose, humming. Meditation is controlling the mind so that you can zero in on the noise it creates. For most of us, when we start or return after an extended break, it takes some time to clear out the clutter. When I'm working with someone who is having mental health concerns or insomnia, my first question is, "How often do you meditate?" Most times it's never, not enough, or "I can't, my brain is too busy."

Meditation takes practice. The more you focus and toss what's in the mind that's not helping you live, the more space is created. *Can't* means this is an area that needs work, and you don't want to put in the work to change. Nothing is impossible unless we make the choice not to try to create change. Stop saying "I can't." You can; you just choose not to.

The Voice of Knowledge by Don Miguel Ruiz provides my favourite visual journey through a biblical story I love about Adam and Eve. It took me a few years and many audiobooks to realized that meditation isn't just sitting on a cushion. It isn't easy to tame my squirrels; after a few minutes, my body starts to ache, then I start to squirm. I spent a couple of decades contorting my life to fit others' expectations, in addition to the fear of their disappointment. That requires more grounding than a booty pillow can offer.

My meditation journey started with learning to connect to my physical body, then connecting my physical body and breath. A logical way of viewing my health came when I learned we have five bodies. In Eastern practices, the five bodies are referred to as *koshas*. One by one, I've have reconnected with these bodies:

- physical (Annamaya)
- breath (Pranamaya)
- mental (Manomaya)
- emotional (Vijnanamaya)
- bliss/spiritual (Anandamaya)

Time and practice have allowed me the opportunity to clear the cobwebs and throw out the garbage that is no longer serving me. When in balance, it is easier to focus on gratitude and my connection with my God (bliss) body. Eastern practices call this *meditation*; my Catholic upbringing calls this *prayer*. While many who knew me growing up think I am dabbling with the devil, this journey and activities like yoga, Reiki, and meditation have brought me closer to God.

Children are designed to play, dream, move, and create. Instead, they are told to sit down and compete. The system (school, state, and church) is designed to strip the spirit from children so that they will become obedient, conforming adults.

Kids really are our best teachers, whether they are ours or we borrow them. We break them with our judgments, threats, and stories. For generations, we expected them to be seen but not heard. We have taught them their voice does not matter. They are told they are too young to take part in society's activities and too old to believe in something unseen. We reward them for being good and punish them for not meeting our expectations, instilling fear.

Consider what would happen to our society if we let 13-year-olds continue playing dress-up instead of assuming that pretending to be a dog was some kind of sexual fetish. How would our world be if we let children retain their innocence instead of assuming and sexualizing their imagination because they hit the age of hormonal fluctuation? My studies have shown me that the human brain doesn't fully develop until around twenty-five. This means everything before twenty-five are our impressionable years. By twenty-five, a majority of people have direction in life: careers, family.

What if my studies are wrong? Science has been wrong before. What if the brain is impressionable as long as we continue to increase our frequency and heal, removing all limits and logical reason? It's this thought that I've put into my daily practice, and has helped me heal what society has restricted.

The solution to fixing the world is to first fix our minds. We have become too knowledgeable. We need to un-educate and become the child who knew anything was possible.

Chapter 13

WAVES OF GRIEF

Grief never goes away. At first, you feel forced to ride the waves of emotion. But over time, you learn it's okay to sit back, watch, and choose which waves are worth your time and energy.

Death and funerals growing up were just as much a part of my youth as weddings and babies. In addition to a pet burial—the hamster my sister loved to death and we buried in the alley—there were many human funerals we had to attend. After Dad's funeral, I took a break and to some extent denied death.

Until Dad, it was simple: they were just people I knew who had gone on to a better place called *heaven*. That's how the Catholic school teaches it. There are only two places to go when you die: heaven or hell. Since none of these people were bad, they must be good; ergo, they went to some kind of utopia.

From Dad's diagnosis to years after his death, I was sent on a quest to understand why we worshiped some man in a white robe who could not even show his presence so sent his only son. Hey, wait, are we not all children of God? It says so in the book that the church endorses.

There were many contradictions in this book (Bible) and the

Catholic Church, and the concept of God had become very fuzzy to me with the death of Dad. Now, before I upset my Catholic or Christian readers, I never abandoned God. In fact, my journey helped me find a stronger connection. This is exactly how life works: grief, love, growth. Change does not happen overnight. It happens in stages.

Time is a construct we have created with sundials, clocks, and calendars. But without these tools, the past, present and future would still exist.

We humans like to create order in the physical world. Grief blows our rational understanding of an organized model away. The sun would still rise and set, the seasons would still change. We are physical beings, living a physical existence, and we want an understanding of everything in a physical terms. We know that when a physical being is born, eventually the physical being will die. The figure *God* helps us to explain why someone is born and why they die. It also gives us something (someone) to hold responsible and explain a birth or death. The idea of *God* creates a logical reason and a being responsible for things that can't be explained.

Spirituality is not the same as religion. Spirituality is knowing there is something bigger than oneself. Choices should be made from the heart and for the betterment of humanity. One is part of the whole; I am the micro within the macro. Religious organizations guide, organize, and create judgment. Someone's life choices will be either seen as good or bad by the religious faith and will be rewarded to heaven or punished to hell.

Where would the man in a white robe send a father who was abused and neglected as a child, who because of his life choices or God's inability to help the man make better choices for his family left them with mountains of debt and years of unresolved resentment? The closest I saw God in my father's life was when he was forced to attend a baptism or wedding. I have memories of him going to church where the best part of the hour-plus service was Dad spitting the host into a napkin.

He prayed all the time—"God dammit!"—out of frustration and anger. He never killed anyone that we know of, but there are a few of the Ten Commandments that he broke. Does he still get into heaven? Is he still worthy? Where was this God to help my father as a child? Why didn't He support him to get back on track as a youth? What kind of God would end a man's life at 48, after stripping him of everything?

I no longer refer to the idea of God as having a body. God is not a *him* or *her* or any other pronoun or title. For me, God is not something one can explain with words or a space; it is something one feels a connection to. God power is bigger than what any church has tried to teach. It is within and connects us all.

When someone moves away, we miss them. It hurts, but we can physically pick up a phone and contact them. Death is a relocation from the physical. The death of my dad has shown me that while his physical meat suit could no longer house the energy his life collected, his soul cannot be destroyed. He has moved past what our physical senses can experience.

The soul is pure energy, and energy cannot be created or destroyed, only transformed. The soul is pure energy. Death is simply vacating the physical vessel so that it can continue to grow without limits. Through the rest of the book, you will see how even though physically my dad is not present in body, his presence is a huge part of my growth. I know my dad is around through signs and feelings.

Like many people, I found comfort in the poem "Footprints in the Sand." It helps me to accept that I wasn't really alone in the darkest time of my life. Unfortunately, I discovered that the poem's ownership is inconclusive, and therefore I could not include it. Imagine multiple individuals having the same experience to share, all of whom needed guidance ending in a court tug of war for copyright authority. This story (poem) is meant to be shared and to heal people. It is part of the oldest story written down long before copyright law.

> *To know that no matter what, no matter where, no matter when, Jesus will never leave us nor forsake us.*—Hebrews 13:5

In the good times, he walks right beside us, and in the bad, he carries us. We are never left alone in this world. We may be in it, but we are definitely not *of* it (John 15:19).

Chapter 14

HEALING THE
PARENTAL WOUND

*When you look at someone through rose-colored
glasses, all the red flags just look like flags.—BoJack
Horseman (Lisa Kudrow as Wanda Pierce)*

My father was an alcoholic, and my mother was his enabler. He
would let life get the best of him and she would leave and stay in a
women's shelter, only to return after a short time. At some point, she
stopped running and just stood by his side and watched him slowly
fall apart, ready to pick up the pieces left in the wake of each storm.

Dad showed me how cruel life could be, while my mother taught
me I am stronger than I think I am. My mom often gets accused of
viewing life through rose-coloured glasses. I, like her, want to believe
that people care as much about me as I do about them. I do believe
everyone has the potential to be kind. Sadly, it is buried by so much
trauma, they become victims and function in a survivor mentality.

In my father's eyes, I don't think I could do any wrong. Dad
based decisions on facts; what he saw was truth.

I was getting ready for a night out. He came into my room and
dropped a travel-size bottle of mouthwash on the bed, which he'd

found under the car seat. It's kind of a blur as to my response, because at 18 and very single, the explanation was pretty self-explanatory. I wanted fresh breath.

Then he asked, "Was it to hide this?" and dropped an empty beer bottle on the bed beside it. Pure disappointment! Consider that this choice had led him down a path of multiple losses: his job, our home, his retirement. This disappointment was my dad's assumption based on his life. Dad definitely wasn't wearing rose-coloured glasses; he was facing a mirror.

The truth was, I had stopped an ex-boyfriend from drinking and driving. Drunk and horny, he took me up on my offer of a ride home. I force him to dump the rest of his beer, and in the process, he bumped the glove box open and a few unopened tampons popped out and landed on the floor at his feet. The way he freaked out, one would have thought I had tossed a used one onto his lap. In the chaos, the bottle ended up under the seat, and he no longer had any expectation of sex.

Mom and I never saw eye-to-eye until I was well into my thirties. I was a handful, and Mom always said she wished I would have a daughter just like me. Three boys in a four-year window sure has been a lesson in boy drama.

She never condoned staying in an unhealthy relationship. She showed me over and over that when you're knocked down and lose everything, get back up and go again. We talk a lot these days. She could not understand why, despite the mounting evidence, she continued to put herself in positions of letting Dad lose everything, over and over again. What I see is a strong woman who forgets to focus on the changes and growth she did accomplish.

For example, she decided to go back to school with five minor children—not an easy task. She decided to get her nursing degree because this was something she had always wanted to do (work with geriatrics). She discouraged relationships with some of the boys I brought around, largely based on a gut instinct that ultimately kept me safe from them and the world. At the time, I resented her for the discomfort and hardships. But later, I discovered that it was through choices to listen to what was right at the time that she and I had the most growth.

Would she have gone back to school had they not moved to Robsart? Would she have ever gained financial independence? Would she and I have ever developed a relationship like the one we have built? Would I look up to her as much as I do now? What she sees as failure or struggle, I see as an opportunity for changing the karmic code, allowing an easier road for me and my children.

The creation of time logic has become humanity's greatest kryptonite. It has heightened our connection to the past—not only what we wish we could do differently but quantified the time that goes by as it passes. There is a countdown to a future. We expect that just like time, the future is predictable. It's not, and this uncertainty creates fear. We have become so preoccupied with the construct of time, we forget to just enjoy the moment as it is occurring.

Growing up, I would not have admitted I learned a lot from my parents, but kudos to them for their sneaky antics: most of my core values are a result of what they taught me. Dad was very logical, while Mom listened more to her heart than her head. Because of them, I will not walk away from a challenge. If I say I can't, I've already failed. Rather, I say, "Challenge accepted," in the voice of Barney from *How I Met Your Mother*.

I know that every time I fail or fall, there is a lesson to be learned. I can always get back up, because I am stronger than I think I am. Sometimes there are a lot of lessons, but it is through watching and experiencing life with my parents that I can confidently keep growing. They did the best they could given what they learnt from their parents. I will do the same, and one day my children will see this and repeat the cycle.

Chapter 15

WARRIOR VERSUS VICTIM

The biggest difference between a warrior and a victim
is that the victim represses and the warrior refrains.—
Don Miguel Ruiz, The Four Agreements

If you're looking for a great audiobook on recognizing your patterns and making new ones, download anything by Don Miguel Ruiz Sr. or his son, Don Miguel Ruiz Jr. Both these men teach and offer beautiful imagery through stories, some based on their lives, others fictional.

The above quote is what propelled me forward. Metaphorically, it ripped open the Pandora's box containing my life's potential. Yoga made me feel strong, but inside I was a mess of a small child doing as I was told. Emotion is not a sign of weakness. It's a sign that the body has had enough and is waving a white or red flag. Emotions are pure energy being released.

Victims come in different forms. We all have that "Debbie Downer" (sorry to all the Debbies, I know a few really great ones). This is the stereotyped victim we all recognize. But how about that insecure manipulator? Did you realize that the same gifts that allow an empath to feel another's pain and heal is what sociopaths, psychopaths, and narcissists use to hurt people?

I dislike the word *toxic* when referring to people; I prefer *broken*. So often, I hear clients talk about their toxic partners, family members, co-workers, and friends. Generation after generation, society has been labelling and diagnosing toxic people as narcissistic, psychopathic, or even a sociopath. Some get locked up, and smaller offenders may choose or be forced to medicate, but for the most part, toxic people continue to partake in our day-to-day, spreading their poor behaviour and attitudes into future generations like a disease.

Toxic creates a picture in my mind of a skull and crossbones, denoting something the effects of which will likely kill you. Society stores this toxic garbage in concrete rooms buried underground for some future generation to deal with. It's not cleaned up; it's just hidden, out of sight, out of mind. Then one day, the concrete gives way and the groundwater is polluted. Life in the area ceases, because society finds it too hard to deconstruct the toxins.

This system is broken! The system of chemical disposal is just how we in society treat the humans we see as waste. Granted, some who walk the earth are beyond help in this life, but some growth is better than no growth. My thought is that by continuing to label and lock up and not actually provide agents of change, we are telling society it is acceptable for people to be broken. This results in the continued growth of human waste. As with chemical waste, human waste will end humanity if we don't deconstruct the monsters we are making.

People who are empathetic have not been given a gift. They become empathetic as a means of survival in a home environment that is dependant on the ability to determine who or what is a threat, and where to find safety. I have yet to meet a client who can't relate to the story of being able to feel the mood in the room, or know how someone feels without them saying a word. Everyone has the ability to pick up on the feelings of others.

Feelings are also known as *emotion*. Think of this as *E-motion*: energy in motion. So if everyone has the ability to read the emotion or energy of others, is it not fair to say everyone has the ability to be an empath? Personal choice and awareness is what prevents people from using their abilities differently—empathic versus narcissistic. Individuals who use empathy for their own sinister pleasure would be sociopaths and psychopaths.

It is research on these types of individuals that has led to the belief that people are a product of both nurture and nature. By saying an individual is born (nature) with neurological (neutron) irregularities, is that not the same as saying they are energetically irregular? The energy has caused disease by turning off their ability to care for their victims.

While we are less likely to know or run into a sociopath or a psychopath and live to talk about it, we all know at least one narcissist and probably more. In fact, I believe we all have the ability to have narcissistic thoughts, just perhaps haven't acted on them. Narcissism ranges in intensity, but generally it involves the use of empathy to manipulate, not physically harm.

Narcissism is the perfect example of what a vampire is from stories—individuals who suck the life slowly out of another human. Being in a relationship with a narcissist is being in a relationship with someone who steals your energy. You either learn to recognize and get out, or your life force (energy) continues to diminish to the point that your light goes out.

A *empathic* person uses trauma to grow. A *narcissist* uses trauma to continue the cycle of pain. The choice of how a person uses their empathetic abilities will either be a gift or a curse to humanity.

From my experience, nothing frustrates narcissists more than when they can feel the power of a heart that loves unconditionally, but they can't manipulate it. They try, they fail, they get really angry. I know I can comfortably sit back sending love from afar that they need to heal. So far, they all just eventually go off and try to steal someone else's light.

When I started to increase my frequency, it brought all kinds of narcissistic creatures from the shadows. I did have to experience the draining of my energy a few times. I learned from clients that it's necessary to cut ties both physically as well as energetically. If they aren't willing to make a change, I have the power to discontinue services.

This I now carry forward into personal relationships, whether with friends or family. My circle or tribe has gotten much smaller, but my sense of fulfilment in the quality of life is greater. Quality over quantity is always a better goal.

I do see both Debbie Downers and insecure manipulators in life and professionally. I have learned I need to be upfront and honest. When I say, "I need to take a break from our relationship so we can continue to love each other from afar," it's not done to be mean or rude. It's simply saying we need space from each other to explore how to grow without one another.

I don't think narcissists are *evil*; this is society's judgment of good versus bad. I don't even think many victims—this includes manipulators—realize the effects of their behaviour on others. The relationships have just become codependent on each other for love as well as abuse.

Clients who come to see me eventually are all faced with the fact that they need to choose change. This realization creates discomfort. Discomfort, no matter the body (physical, mental, emotional, breath, or bliss), is a sign of growth potential. Realizing that I was strong enough to bring about that much discomfort in so many people helped me understand my ability to be a catalyst for change.

I can't change everyone. But those who choose to shine a light on their personal dark spaces can grow.

I'm a boy mom, and superheroes have been a big part of our home since 2007. We have created names for each of our family members: Macman, Bonk, Famous, Nova, and I'm M (mother), the woman who gets the crew out the door and on their daily missions. We are all unique, and the caricatures my younger sister drew for each of the boys' fourth birthday solidifies their personalities into superhero-dom.

I love the frequent question asked in our house: "What would your superpower be?" My youngest has learned to tailor the question to an either/or because you can never have too many superpowers, right?

But I don't need to wish for a superpower: I have one. I always have, even before knowing about my gifts. As a teen, I remember sitting in my boyfriend's car feeling out the house to see if my parents were up. I was always happy when Mom had gone to bed and Dad had taken over her watch. His concern was more manageable than Mom's fury.

As I have come into understanding how emotions work, I have learned how to use them to protect and serve myself and others in my life. When you have power over your emotions, you can influence those around you, provided your energy exchange is welcomed. From experience, I've learned caution must be practised. If I continue to give, give, give without a source to replenish my energy, over time, I will feel defeated.

I choose who I surround myself with, and if someone is an energetic drain, it is I who have the power to make the choice to step away personally or professionally. A hero like a healer must know when it's time to turn back to base and replenish. I own my darkness and will not blame something else. Every time I make the choice to listen to my heart, I embody my inner warrior.

Fate whispers to the warrior,
"You can not withstand the storm."
The warrior whispers back,
"I am the storm."
—Unknown

Chapter 16

SETTING BOUNDARIES

It is your choice: will life be heaven or hell?

Definitely the hardest part of the healing process is setting boundaries. Every empathic person is drawn to the most broken people, and there is a need to fix their problems and take their pain away. No matter how many times we are told that others are not our problem to fix, the need is like a drug, and we will often sacrifice ourselves in attempting this impossible task. First, we must learn to love ourselves; then loving others comes naturally.

The day I discovered Reiki, I felt at my lowest. Three weekends into YTT, so many past wounds I had buried resurfaced. I cried uncontrollably and had no idea where to even begin. Somehow I made my way to a local crystal shop, sobbing, and asked for an emotional cleanse. Kinda funny that the man who came to the front looked a lot like Jesus with a ponytail and tie-dyed T-shirt and shorts. I wanted to laugh, but the tears just kept flowing.

This was my intro to Reiki. Immediately, I wanted to know more about this man's magic. As fate would have it, a friend of a friend knew someone, and *boom*, I registered and started my Reiki journey.

Level one was all about self-love. First you must heal yourself, then you are capable of helping others in their healing.

Level one teaches grounding and introduces awareness. In my course, I added in basic chakra information as well as introduction to intuition (clairs). Where William Rand's teachings focus on hands-on practices, my teaching is more focused on energetic understanding. Another way of putting it: I use *his-story* (historic Reiki teachings/masculine practices), add in *my-story* (applied and used to heal my energetics, feminine practices), to help my students discover *their-story* (practices that work for their unique bodies).

The majority of people are looking for a quick fix, like popping a pill. Energy work is a method I've discovered takes longer to see results, but over the long term creates an irreversible upgrade of life quality. What took years to develop in the body will take just as long, if not longer, to undo.

If you participate in a practice—yoga, Reiki, Ayurveda, or any other magical practice—once a week, it will help you for the day. If you can incorporate a practice twice a week, you will start to notice changes in one or more of your bodies (koshas). If you can incorporate a practice three or more times a week, your bodies will start to crave the practice, and it will become a lifestyle you are trying to create versus just a practice. The closer you come to making your practice a lifestyle, the more your frequency will increase, bringing you closer to equaling and embodying pure love.

Unfortunately, the brighter you shine, the more bugs you will attract. Learning to create boundaries to protect your newly created shine is not only necessary but mandatory for you to keep growing.

The only people who get upset when you set boundaries are the ones who benefited from you having none.—Unknown

There are many kinds of pests that try to steal your light. They start to appear as soon as you start to make a change. You'll notice tension within close relationships. Keep in mind you will either inspire their growth or attract new friendships. Every person you meet, you will forever have an emotional attachment to. The stronger the relationship once was, the greater the cord between you and another will be.

You'll likely run into people you haven't seen in years. It will start as a funny coincidence, but it will become unavoidable. This is because these are energetic cords that you are outgrowing. Think of it as your past that you have tried to outrun catching up with you. Many of these people on an unconscious level are seeking out reconnection because you both haven't quite grasped the lessons you were meant to learn from your time together.

If you do manage to avoid them, you will continue to bring the same people in until you finally face what you are avoiding. You can't outrun the lessons you came here to learn. They will be tools for something bigger that you are a part of at a later date.

Other people will attempt to humble you by belittling what you are accomplishing or making fun of your new life and practices. Create boundaries in the form of how much energy you are willing to invest. By walking away, creating those lines of what is acceptable and not, you starve them of their energetic source: you. They'll either look for a new energetic host or be forced to assess their own life patterns and choices.

Energetic growing pains can be very uncomfortable, but they are intended to bring you into balance and closer to the purpose you are here to complete. Take a big breath and put up a barrier, knowing you are protecting your energy and possibly forcing them to grow as well.

My kids taught me that having the ability to laugh when life is uncomfortable gives you your power back. Fear is driven by a lack of understanding of that which is unknown. Those who don't understand often are not ready to learn. Remember, the only person you can change is yourself. So if they aren't ready to explore something other than what they have been programmed to remember, they are only fearing the unknown.

I was raised in a Roman Catholic home and have had many friends and family share their concern for my eternal soul. I tell them, "I'll be careful and be sure to fill my heart with love and not darkness." One would never think that stretching would allow the soul to be exposed to the devil, so why yoga? Because the name of the practice is written in many religious documents as a dark art.

I never get defensive or offended. However, laughter is a frequent thought each time I am told about the dangers of yoga, Reiki, and meditation. How could loving myself and using self-care practices be evil? I encourage those who want to make a practice out of taking care of your mental, emotional, or physical health to just smile if others deem it evil. Continue to love yourself—and them for their concern.

I'm still regularly prayed for, which I graciously accept, because I know their prayers, (meditation with intention) come from a place of love. It just helps my light get brighter.

Setting boundaries, I've discovered, is a form of rebelling against others' expectations. There's no way to sugar-coat boundaries. Sometimes they really suck due to the bout of emotional pain required to create them. It feels like we have to say goodbye oftentimes to people we have been told never to hurt, or have an obligation to treat with respect and kindness no matter what. But I'm happy to say that in most cases, the people I have had to create boundaries around eventually came around and changed. Do it out of love, for yourself as well as the person who needs the boundary. When you create boundaries, you allow yourself to heal.

Visualize for a minute a child who repeatedly falls and skins his knees. As long as he continues to skateboard or bike, he will continue to rip open the wound, and it won't heal. As a parent, I can take comfort in knowing there is a seasonal solution here in Canada. Winter will come, and my child's knee will have a good six to eight months to repair. The tissue will grow back a little thicker to prepare for next year's trauma.

If you continue to expose yourself, or perhaps your children, to belittling, negativity, and judgment, not only will you and they become emotionally calloused, you'll never full heal. The source of your pain has never gone away. Every time you experience these people, it will set you back, again and again. Setting boundaries lets them know that you don't want to be around them, and/or there are limits to being in your presence.

You are being an agent for growth by creating boundaries. You are taking time and space to heal and grow. You are also providing them with time and space to heal and grow. In time, many will chose change because living without you is unbearable.

Setting boundaries is the superior form of self-protection. You are precious, and nobody can protect you better than you. Through boundaries, you teach those who feel the walls you've built how you deserve to be loved.

Let the creation of boundaries come from a place of love. Set your intention to "see you later," not "final farewell." Make it a clean send-off, not a nasty breakup.

When I left home, my mom offered me great advice that I often think about when I decide it's time for an energetic break. The day I left home at 18, I was really grouchy. My mom told me not to make it easy for her to see me go, because it will be harder when it's time to come back.

There have been people who have been nasty! When one friend couldn't convince me that Riley had stolen a phone at her husband's funeral, she turned it around and accused me of stealing it. She told me that I was a disgusting person for letting Riley take the blame. She continued to rattle on about how she regretted bringing me into her life, and that I had to cut ties with all our mutual friends.

Words of fire! I reminded her that I still loved her and that one day, she would know I never did these things. Then I said, "Please do not contact me again." I have no regrets, and one day she will see I was innocent and what really went down. Knowing she has no power over me, my boundary keeps me present on my mat, even when she shows up at the same class I have signed up for.

It's near impossible to build boundaries to protect your whole world. At the very least, your home should be a place where you feel total safety. If something were to push you down through the day, you know you would have someplace to fall at the end.

We may be able to choose our friends, but family is forever. Some days, it feels unfortunate, but there is a blood connection. That is something we can't change or stop.

I have heard firsthand stories of transplant recipients who developed cravings or had memories after their procedure that weren't theirs. So think about it ... family comes from the same life source. You can never completely get rid of someone when you share this connection. This is why the hurt they inflict stings so much more.

Cutting them out is essentially just running away, so instead, create a boundary. Some boundaries may last the rest of a lifetime, but energetically, you're ending on a note of love and hope instead of hate and resentment. Love is higher in frequency, allowing the body to heal and you to continue your journey of personal growth.

Chapter 17

HEALING EMOTIONAL PATTERNS

I use to get offended when someone said I was acting crazy.
Now I thank them for noticing that I'm not normal.

Little by little, I discovered that as boundaries went up, some in response turned them into walls. However, within my new walls, I found so many people like me, wanting to live life with love and compassion and provide support. Some change has been easy and appeared to happen overnight. Other changes have been painful.

A metaphor many refer to, and I absolutely love, is that growth is like peeling away layers of an onion. The first layer was fun and painless. Since that first layer, the layers have come off in chunks and with tears.

There have been so many tears working through the layers. If you stop, the exterior dies and dries. The onion will either sprout new life or it will rot. Just like the choice toward spiritual growth, you continue to put in the energy to grow or disease sets in.

I've always been a crier. Not that I was comfortable crying; I just couldn't refrain from crying. If I was sad, I would cry. Happy cry, scared cry, angry cry—I realize that even though I cried, I never resolved many of the underlying reasons that caused the emotions. It was the quote by Don Miguel, "a warrior refrains, never represses," that will forever turn the lights on when I choose to go back into the dark.

It was during some journaling that the memory of my time working at city hall as a planner came back to me. There were many times when I would get so mad at my supervisor, the planning commission, the city elected officials, I would get to the point of checking out. I bit my cheeks to the point I could taste blood to prevent exploding into tears of rage. There were at least three times I lost control when I was forced to respond.

My job was to follow a book of official guidelines—bylaws. However, my research supporting denials of approval was constantly overturned. I would be instructed to sign my name on permits that did not meet the bylaw standards. My credibility was being sacrificed due to some person higher up the ladder making their own rules.

Usually I could hold back the tears repressing emotions like anger and resentment. I never learned to forgive how that place made me feel, because I never learned how to release. Once again, my kids saved me. Everyone has met kids who, when in trouble, will laugh. When they laugh, it makes you even more angry, or at least it used to, until I decided to join in.

I learned that the emotions I repressed were a result of the judgment I felt from the outside world and as the only woman in a male-dominated workplace. I did see tempers get hot over my short employment there, but I wasn't about to show anger myself. The last thing I wanted to do was cry, so I attempted to repress.

When my son Nathan started to smirk when he was in trouble, I put myself in his shoes. There were so many reasons he could be laughing. Was it a result of how I looked at the moment? This is only ego-based reasoning. Any person who listens to their ego will only get more angry in this scenario. Or was his laughter because he knew what he did wasn't a smart choice, and he laughed because he got caught. Not only is laugher contagious, it heals.

I learned to release the resentment and anger I had toward so many past experiences through laugher, including but not limited to my time working as a city planner. When faced with situations that bring about anger, I now acknowledge the feelings I am experiencing, then try to see it from their eyes. With a clear mind, it's amazing how often I can move past the event. Sometimes a chuckle sneaks out, or a spirited remark, but I no longer repress. Those who want to judge will; that's the beauty of free will. However, free will is a double-edged sword. You can use it to slay your demons or be sacrificed.

I tell my boys, "If the choice was to have the world think I was crazy or have people like me. I'd pick *crazy* every time. Being crazy is less lonely. I know crazy means at least I love myself."

Chapter 18

BLOOMING IMAGINATION
AND INTUITION

While city kids were busy playing boyfriend and girlfriends at
ten years old, I was able to build forts in a ghost town, located
between here and nowhere for three additional years.

As I have mentioned, I was raised Roman Catholic. Not the kind of
Catholic that attended Sunday school every Sunday; however, I do
remember a few weekends of dressing up and having to sit still on
uncomfortable burgundy chairs or a hard oak pew. The exit-stage-
right was the school gymnasium.

In my younger years, it was here that I was allowed to hear
stories of events that happened a long time ago, far, far away. We
would draw and colour pictures of amazing heroes like Jesus, God
his father, and a couple of amazing women both named Mary.
Twice a year, we would put on a play re-enacting these stories. Being
blonde, I usually got typecast into the role of an angel, except for
that one year I got to play Jesus's mother at Christmas.

I'm so grateful for these experiences, because I do believe they
helped shape my ability to see, hear, and connect with energy. Think
about it: books (scrolls) written many lifetimes ago were found,

translated, and are used to worship a man who even the people who wrote the books never personally met. Yet millions follow the words in these books blindly because "this is the word of the Lord, Jesus Christ." Thanks to my intuitive gifts, I don't have to believe blindly. I know J.C. has my back.

I am grateful for the home I grew up in. Exposure to the Bible stories, Santa, the Easter bunny, and the tooth fairy allowed me to use my imagination to create that which I could not see. My kids gave me the opportunity to pass the torch and reconnect with these figures. I chose to baptise my boys and enrolled them into the Catholic school system. We welcomed a mysterious couple of elves over the years into our home, and we all partake in their adventures now that the boys are older.

This is the first ingredient to intuition: imagination. It can be fact, fiction, or a blend of both. In order to *see*, one has to create, out of blind trust, that which is truth.

Magic Is the Ability to Believe, Without Seeing Why or How It Happened

Most days, I'd have to give credit to my boys for saving me. Without them and their imaginations, I don't think I would have realized that my intuition or gifts even existed.

I remember the first psychic I went too: Stampede 2006. I walked past the tent a few times until my timing was perfect and nobody would see me in line. I'd had a miscarriage only a few months earlier, and on that morning I'd taken a pregnancy test and it was positive. I hadn't told a soul, not even Riley.

I don't think my butt had even landed in the seat when the elderly lady announced, "You're with child!" I felt my whole body melt into the chair beneath me as the fear of another loss left. I had no idea at that time that I would be in that lady's shoes saying words of magic to help others. But here I am living the dream.

I'm no Hollywood witch, but I have found it fun to embrace this social label. Like the song "W.I.T.C.H." by Devon Cole says, I am a "women in total control of herself." Life is short. Have fun, learn to laugh, and see the unknown as magical.

Fear is the path to the Dark Side. Fear leads to anger,
anger leads to hate, hate leads to suffering.—Yoda

I frequently get complimented on my home. Despite three teenage boys and a small petting zoo of critters, my house is clean and not at all scary (unless it's past the boys' bedtime). It is welcoming to anyone who crosses the threshold. On nearly every flat surface, you'll find pretty rocks. I also have custom art, including a broom above my front door called "Crystal's Cruiser." To the right, you'll see a red sparkly pointed hat I made last year for Halloween but thought was too beautiful to box and put away. So now it sits on top of a large amethyst cathedral.

Looking around, you'll see many fairy tale items. Some you'd have to be blind to miss, like a large crystal ball, a teacup (*Alice in Wonderland*), and an immortal rose (*Beauty and the Beast*). My kitchen proudly showcases a cauldron for burning, an assortment of herbs, and plenty of homemade candles. Crystals spill into my sleep haven (bedroom); in addition, a huge dream catcher hangs from the ceiling, and witching bells sit above the door.

Vintage mason jars of moon water fill the windowsill in different counts, depending on what I'm called to use between moon phases. Don't be surprised to see herbs marinating in the sunlight with some kind of liquid for a body rub, tincture, or tonic. Most days, I add to the atmosphere (rather than mask the additional inhabitant smells) with oils, sage, or a home-cooked meal.

I prefer colour to black and unicorns to ravens. I laugh when the first-impression bubble is popped and my students and clients or even family realize the real me. On the surface, I'm this down-to-earth yogi who fluctuates in appearance from homeless to yummy mommy. If I was to draw a caricature of my superhero self, it would be cross between Glinda (the good witch in *The Wizard of Oz*) and Rainbow Brite, with the muscles and power of Thor.

It doesn't happen overnight. There is no one book that will give you the ability to manifest or perform miracles, create a spell, or mix magic. There is no hocus pocus, voodoo, or wishing with a chicken bone that will give you unrestricted power over the universe. As the layers of your metaphoric onion are peeled and love increases from within, you start noticing little things—synchronicities. The more attention you pay by being present, the more the frequency and power behind these synchronicities increases.

Then, out of nowhere, it's like the switch has been flipped, and I'm that scared little girl hiding in the bathroom, feet up on the toilet so the mean girls don't find me. This is visiting the dark! I don't see a man in a red suit or a black cloak. It's me triggered by past wounds, falling, victim.

Children Know What They Want to Be When They Grow Up: Happy

Every time the darkness from within reappears, I feel powerless. In yoga teacher training, I gave my darkness (ego) a name. I encourage you to try to do this as well. "Pam," in my imagination, looks like the character Pamela Anderson played in the '90s version of Baywatch, a more modern-day Marilyn Monroe—a bodacious blonde, much like myself, and the wounded child within could not help but relate our physical qualities.

No, I don't have an imaginary friend named Pam; she is my voice of ego. The voice of fear, created by society, on what I need to do or be in order to fit in and be loved. It is the creation or tool I call Pam that has allowed me to successfully sort through the feelings of my ego (society expectation) and intuition (direction to my soul's purpose).

I have heard frequently from councillors and teachers the importance of revisiting and healing the inner child in order to move forward and be happy. Without imagination, it is my belief that one will not hear intuition. So I use my imagination to give form to my inner child.

When I discovered I could not remove this part of who I am, I made Pam my friend. I now acknowledge what this part of me has to say, experience the feelings associated with Pam's opinions, and work toward a compromise provided Pam (fear) continues to listen to my heart. Pam's advice keeps me safe, and my heart (love) keeps me moving in the direction of my soul's purpose.

We have been taught to blame rather than take responsibility. "The devil made me do it." No, *your* free will made you do it. Pam allows me to acknowledge that maybe my decision wasn't the wisest choice, but it was still me that made it.

Chapter 19

FINDING DAD IN ROBSART

I was born on the prairies where the wind blew free
and there was nothing to break the light of the sun.
I was born where there were no enclosures.
—Geronimo (1829–1909)

By January 2017, my body hurt all the time, which made it hard to
work out and lose the weight I had gained post–kidney removal. My
doctor kept pushing pills to "support" my remaining kidney, despite
test results saying my remaining kidney was doing its job.

My marriage was starting to have some significant fault lines as a
result of Riley constantly comparing us to the Joneses. He panicked
nearly every day about our finances. It was the first and last thing
he looked at in bed. Since I didn't make the money, I felt I had to
ask for permission anytime I made a purchase, including groceries.

My babies, by 2017, were not so much babies anymore, rather
becoming independent and vocal preteens. The introduction of
hormones and personality differences led to many arguments among
the men in the house, big and small. I was feeling lonely despite the
very loud house I lived in. It's sad how blind an individual becomes.
In an attempt to hold on to the life that was once comfortable,

despite it no longer existing, I stood on a metaphoric cliff debating whether to jump. I went to bed many nights praying to not wake up and cried the next morning because I had to do it all over.

I talked to professionals but would not classified myself as suicidal during that time. I would never intentionally hurt myself; my boys needed me. But I hoped and even prayed that my time would just be done. I wanted outside confirmation from God that I had accomplished what I was supposed to and it was just my time.

I had not worked as a city planner for about seven years when I reapplied and was denied in 2017. Around this time, I had seen that a local yoga studio I practiced at was offering a two-hundred-hour yoga teacher training program. So I decided to enrol because maybe it was time for a career change.

Riley was impressed with the idea of a job with flexibility, so he fronted the money. I also made a second attempt, three months after my first attempt with the city, when the guy they had hired decided to take a job in a bigger centre. The city offered excellent income, and with money I felt I had the opportunity for independence and happiness. However, the second application went just as well as the first one.

Twice I had been shortlisted, and the position was given to some guy who had never been to the city. Both times the person they chose instead of me left approximately three months after being hired. It made me laugh, and I didn't want to be part of this toxic cycle anymore.

Burning time and money are not the same.
Man can always make more money.

Summer 2017

I stretched my wings and decided to attend a family reunion at a ranch house just outside Cypress Hills, Saskatchewan. I had never done a trip without Riley, let alone a full weekend trip with the three boys.

I remembered going to reunions with my dad even after I left home. Dad would haul his truck out with a ratty truck trailer on the back. He'd introduce me to my great aunts and uncles, the families who raised him from this age to that, and the farms he worked at to save and buy items like his first cowboy boots. He repeated his stories and introductions multiple times over the weekend, partially because he was excited to share me, but mostly because he was intoxicated.

I rented the room in the ranch house and spent the weekend making memories with my boys. They ran wild, got filthy, suffered some minor injuries, and made new friends. Even though Dad wasn't there to do the introductions, I was welcome and remembered. I wasn't lonely; it was as if dad was with me that whole trip.

We stuck around until the end, helping to clean up the ranch house and grounds. There was no rush to head home. I wasn't ready for the weekend to be done. So I decided to pack up and make a detour in the opposite direct of home to my old stomping grounds of Robsart. My dad's younger brother, my uncle, lived there, and he reminded me so much of my dad.

It was a short visit. We walked up and down the dirt streets observing what buildings were gone and the few that still stood. I was amazed by their deterioration over approximately twenty-five years since I was last there. We planned a few more visits before winter set in and stayed in my uncle's trailer while it was warm enough.

Unfortunately, winters in Robsart bring lots of snow and freezing temperatures, which made it impossible to continue visits through Christmas into the New Year. But as soon as the snow melted, the boys and I were back out there again.

Getting out with nature and away from people creates a clearer connection with earth through the elements. Earth, not concrete. Water in from lakes and steams. Air uninterrupted by concrete and steel. Fire created, or the sun. Ether from the stars, more visible without street lights.

Spring 2018

I allowed my boys the opportunity to experience life the way most city kids are robbed of. Our first trip out that year was in early April. I didn't plan ahead and was hit by a spring storm about thirty minutes from Robsart.

My aunt had called me and let me know that my uncle had been up all night because many of his cattle had decided it was a great time to give birth. Unfortunately, they aren't financially well off, which meant that their house sometimes doubled as a place to keep calves warm while they dried after birth. That morning, they had three black troughs that were doubling as nurseries. One of the calves succumbed to the effects of the cold.

My boys inspected all three baby cows, even the dead one. It isn't just a little boy thing. I remember as a kid finding a dead bird under the deck and making it a house by stacking small pieces of lumber left over from my dad's garage build. We watched as the first calves made their way back to their mama, and we dried more calves before feeding them their first meal. We experienced life, death, and everything in between.

Spring in the city is marked by the appearance of street sweepers replacing the plows. Spring in the country has new life around every corner. In May 2018, we snuck out for another visit. This time, I discovered that a couple of the buildings were for sale. One was the old mayor's office/firehall. The other was a dilapidated warehouse/shop.

My imagination started to run wild as the thought of creating a home away from home filled my mind. It started off small but grew as I shared my vision with friends. Before I knew it, I was planning future retreats in a ghost town. I finally concluded that my visions were too big for a city planner. They may have decided I wasn't the right fit to design their city, and perhaps that's because my purpose was bigger. So, fine. I'm going to design my own town.

A successful life is a happy life. For me, it can be
measured each day by the amount of dirt you wash
from your face—and the smile beneath it all.

I convinced Riley that buying the lots was a good investment. By this time, I had saved up some money from teaching yoga, but I still felt I needed Riley's approval for any big purchases. The lots were less in value than payment for two seasons of trailer-space rental at any of the sites our friends retreated to. The fact that the land would pay for itself in two years helped Riley humour me in my dreams. Worst-case scenario, I could walk away and give the land back to the county.

I called the building owner and asked for a tour. The first building was in better shape but still needed to be gutted. The first would require the removal of many horse trailers of trash. The 2,100-square-foot space was filled with worn-out couches, recliners, chairs, tables, mattresses, carpet, kitchen Tupperware, appliances (big and small), books, clothing, and so much more.

During the tour, I got confirmation that Dad was present. Some call them signs or synchronicities. Sitting on top of a burgundy couch were a pile of eight-tracks and cassettes, some in large cases, others loose. Sitting on top at an awkward angle was a cassette case of John Cougar Mellencamp. I smiled and fought back a tear. "Okay, Dad, I'm home."

We agreed on a price. I went home and collected a cashier's check, and pretty much overnight, I became the proud owner of a slice of land in the middle of nowhere, with nothing around. Before the fall of 2018, with the help of my uncle, we got the one building completely emptied. Demolition started in the spring of 2019, once the rain and snow had stopped.

There were a few hiccups, and additional help was called in with the realization that the building was in worse shape than anticipated. By early August, I was ready to drive out and light a match, I was so frustrated. The contractor sided with the idea of demolition and starting from scratch. His compliance is probably why I got off the phone, took a couple of deep breaths, then told him that was enough for this year. It would definitely be cheaper, but it wouldn't be an authentic ghost-town retreat if the build was new.

The plan was to start again the following spring. However, that spring, the world, not just me, had a big block. In March 2020, COVID shut down the world by chasing everyone to their homes, where they wouldn't kill those most vulnerable. This fear was just the thing needed to create division within my family and the realization that it was space, not people, that healed my soul.

By learning to love yourself, you'll recognize your worth from others. You will know how it feels to be loved unconditionally.

Spring 2020

Thanks to COVID, I had no access to a contractor, so I continued demolition of the interior myself. The money I had saved up over the winter went into running electricity to another lot owned by my dad's sister (my godmother), fixing an old trailer up, and setting up an above-ground pool. While the world shut down, I found joy in my happy place.

It confused most of my family and many friends that I liked Saskatchewan so much. One friend even asked what the attraction was. There was no body of water. I responded, "Where there is water, there are people. I go there because the only noise is the noise of my thoughts … as well as the buzz of power lines on hot days."

Manifestation is creation that happens when you take the step to make dreams a reality. Expecting a divine power to step in and make the dream physical is a dream in itself. You are the divine power, so get to work. Accepting your divinity occurs when you accept you are not alone. Turn in and watch. When the physical clutter clears, there are signs. Our senses have just been too busy to experience or accept them.

It started with music and dreams, then one day, it was as if Dad was right there in the room with me. Now I can request signs for confirmation, comfort, or direction. Through signs, in many ways my dad has helped support me more now than he did when he was alive. If I hit a wall, he sends me a metaphoric hammer to keep me moving forward. My dad has taught me the importance of an open mind and a loud heart.

Chapter 20

GHOSTS OF THE PAST

There is no great genius without a mixture of madness.—Aristotle

I'm no specialist. I haven't spent a ridiculous amount of time and money memorizing books and lectures of others' knowledge. In university, I studied an assortment of humanities: anthropology, psychology, sociology, geography, and history, some more than others. I say I have an undergrad degree in people-watching (BA major in Urban and Regional Studies). I see the patterns in people and society, past, present, and expected future. I not only make the observations, I feel the emotional energy associated with the material.

My mother worked in the local hospital psychiatric wing, so in addition to having the fear of being called crazy by society, I was terrified of a clinical diagnosis like schizophrenia by someone very close to me. They say there is a fine line between love and hate. Both are intense emotions, on opposite sides of the frequency spectrum. The same can be said about madness and genius. In my experience, the cure is grounding. When I bring myself back into balance of the physical body, imagination and intuition are in harmony.

I have met some amazing healers over the years. Problem is, we are all human, and we default to old patterns. Intuitive healers like energy workers (Reiki and prana), psychics, mediums, and shamans are naturally more open to listening to their intuition. Our upper energy centres are more active. Work in the physical centres (below the heart) requires intentional awareness. Imbalance starts by putting others before ourselves—stepping away from our self-care because we see the opportunity to help just one more soul.

Self-care involves all bodies. When one body is out of balance, you can't correct it by putting more effort into another. You can't meditate yourself back to correcting an imbalance in your physical or breath body any more they you can burn off anxiety and depression (emotional and mental body imbalance) by running ten kilometres a day.

Both examples may work as a Band-Aid (a distraction), but continuing these practices over the long term will create greater imbalance between physical and astral (energetic) bodies.

The punishment for being a dreamer is seeing potential without proof. For most, they need to see to believe. I'm a dreamer, so naturally, if left unchecked, I could easily fall into a large number of Western labels for a mental illness: depression (yup), anxiety (been there too), bipolar (happened), schizophrenia (grandmother), ADHD (most definitely). The physical practice of yoga helped me reconnect with my physical body and realize my imagination is a coping tool.

I medicate by putting myself into a food coma. Energetically, the weight gain makes me feel more grounded. But like any addiction, the high wears off, and I'm back to square one. Only this time with guilt, remorse, and a few more pounds.

Too much time in the dream world enables a blurring of the line between conscious and unconscious. Dreams can happen while you're awake (daydreams), resulting in lethargy and furthering the energetic imbalance of the physical body. Even as I sit here and write, I am frequently facing the urge to take a break and run to the store for ice cream and a lotto ticket. Thanks to COVID, I developed a new addiction of buying the occasional ticket to fill the void of not being allowed in yoga studios. Tickets give me the opportunity to dream more, from home renovations to island purchases with private jet access.

When the physical body is neglected, it will continue to be neglected until there is a consciousness about the unhealthy patterns. The dreamer needs to make the choice and adopt a new pattern to correct the imbalance. Not all dreamers use substances like alcohol, gambling, or food. Anything that provides an escape mentality or distraction from reality (physical world) is an addiction. Shopping, listening to music, sex, even meditation can become addictive.

To ground and bring balance into the physical body, one needs to *feel* the body. Intuition and imagination are closely linked, and without physical grounding of the body, the line between the two blurs or completely disappears. I have witnessed these imbalances resulting in psychosis-like symptoms as well as the manifestation of physical disease.

> *We are the granddaughters of the witches they couldn't burn. Women like me whose souls came back to teach you the errors of your ways.—Unknown*

Feminine energy makes women more natural at intuitive healing. I recommend the book *Witches, Midwives, and Nurses: A History of Women Healers* by Barbara Ehrenreich *and* Deirdre English. It's a quick and easy read on the introduction of medicine—a masculine, science-based method of healing—and the elimination of natural or intuitive healing by creation of laws making it illegal. First women were shunned, then persecuted, and finally mass-murdered. Intuition became a death sentence during King James's day and for centuries after as the medical system grew.

The belief still exists in the majority that those educated know more about patients' health than the patients themselves. Are doctors successful 100 per cent of the time? I've watched as many people have blamed medical professionals for mistakes that led to disabilities and even death of their loved ones. In reality, I would say a doctor's decision is based mostly on a textbook answer and little on experience with other patients.

They are educated-guess makers, under the assumption that people are all the same. Therefore, the procedure and the results should be just as constant. The current medical system's ideas that were designed by men and taught to men are very structured and logical, leaving no room for variables like an individual's unique energetics.

I know little about my ancestors other than that their relocation from overseas was always to escape persecution for one reason or another. While I have a deep-rooted urge to run myself, I'm going to have to say the need to fight for my kids' future is even stronger. My mom became a nurse, the first woman in her family to get a piece of credential paper. Before her, my grandmothers were caregivers and homemakers for their families.

I myself knew I didn't want to be a nurse—very few kids will choose to follow in their parents' footsteps. Prior to having children, I could not figure out why anyone in their right mind would procreate in this damaged world. I never dreamed of the wedding, the happily-ever-after. For a planner, I never really had a plan. I joke about having Peter Pan syndrome, and how still, at 43, "When I grow up I want to be a ...." I'm more of a dreamer than a planner. Currently, I'm learning how my past heritage is shaping my present awareness, and I am awaiting the results and future surprises.

Death by fire is no longer a worry for those who use their intuition. A clinical psychosis diagnosis, however, is a modern-day practice that discourages many from exploring or admitting their use of intuitive and energy work. My family has made extended jokes about my "witchy" love of rocks and oils. My knowledge of the iconic symbols and the misunderstanding of the history behind them makes their eyes glaze over, and the topic is quickly dismissed.

Did you know that the five-point star represents the connection between the five elements (air, water, fire, earth, and ether), or that the broom was to sweep out not just the dirt from unwelcome guests but also clean the energetics they brought in with them? My favourite story is definitely the explanation I heard behind the cauldron. Women did the cooking, and since fridges were not yet invented, fermentation was a method of food preservation. One of the many things women fermented was beer, which they sold to taverns. Men in taverns would drink the witches' brew (beer) and do unspeakable acts, then blame the potion and the witches who made it.

I love stories! Whether or not these are fact or fiction, people around me watched as I explored the unknown, enjoying these stories when I shared them.

About three years ago, I attended an online meditation with the intention of connecting with an ancestor. For me, meditation is an opportunity to quiet the noise from the physical world while still consciously listening to my higher power (God/Source/Universe). This energy may come in the form of a memory, a colour, a feeling, or better yet, the energy of a being.

I would never call myself a medium or psychic. I know I've pointed this out a time or two so far in this book, but I'll say it again: by labelling my gifts, I limit them. Psychics read potential energetic outcomes if the events of today do not change. Mediums read the energy of loved ones who no longer are in human form. I open myself to anything.

This particular meditation allowed me the opportunity to hear from my dad's mom. Grandma Helen was diagnosed clinically with schizophrenia in the '50s and never returned home after her eighth child. In this vision, using my mind's eye (not my physical eyes), I heard Grandma say to trust the voices, and the pain would go away.

I felt a coolness wash across my head. I saw her strapped to a bed and electroshock therapy being administered. Then I felt the pain—not my pain but hers. I could feel a tear roll down my cheek and a warm hand wipe it away.

When the meditation was completed, I knew what I needed to

do: trust the inaudible voices, and the cluster headaches I had been having since 2011 with the birth of my third son would go away. Headaches are an inherited disabling disease that runs through my dad's side of the family. I had tried everything from pill, to THC/CBD, even a daith piercing (same results as acupuncture, only more permanent). All had helped reduce the pain. However it was my visit from Grandma and her story that has nearly eliminated them completely.

Now, if I feel the onset of brain pain, my first go-to isn't pills. I brew myself a large mug of hibiscus, mugwort and rose tea and follow it with a meditation. I turn off the noise of the physical world. Sometimes I black out and rest, but more often, I hear a voice or truth I have been ignoring.

When we fully embrace our intuition, the voices, and the stories, there is always fear of judgment. My mom, a retired psych nurse, was my greatest weakness. The day I told her about the meditation and Grandma's words, and how I had applied her story to my life and the success with the reduction of headaches, she smiled, then laughed, and finally commented (in a joking tone), "Honey, you know where I work, right?"

Old me never would have told anyone about my crazy visions, especially someone who could have gotten me committed. Present me knows that there is a fine line between intuition and imagination, much like the line between genius and insanity. Future me hopes that by being open and vulnerable to criticism and judgment, I can help others to trust their intuition.

Be crazy, be stupid, be weird. Be whatever, because life is too short to be anything but happy.—*Unknown*

Chapter 21

CHARLEY

People come into your life because it's part of the bigger design.
The length and frequency they come in and out depends on
how long it takes you to learn what they are there to teach.

Charley walked in to my room on November 6, 2020. I could tell by the way he carried himself that he was in a lot of pain and his body was not cooperating with his mind. There was very little talk that first day. He was on a mission, and he knew from previous experiences with Reiki that it would help with the symptoms of his multiple sclerosis.

He told me of a healer he'd visited in the past who helped him with symptoms. Even though I had a different technique, he was very interested in what I had to say. Since the world shutdown in March 2020, Charley had regressed significantly, and he knew that the energy of the planet was resulting in the progress of his disease.

I could feel an instant energy draw to Charley when we met but couldn't put my finger on why. Something felt very familiar about him. He had been born in Medicine Hat but left as a young teen, moving to Saskatchewan until a couple years ago when he moved to the area with his dad because of his poor health.

I told him how sure I was that we had met before, and that my assumption was we must have known each other in a past life. Partially truth, partially making a joke of the sense of familiarity I felt with him. Ego likes to jump in from time to time, so I'll say things like I'm joking in order to prevent me from coming off like a loony. With Charley, I felt I could be my real, authentic, loony self.

My comment about past lives was well received, and Charley enthusiastically said he believed in "that stuff" too. There was trust, and Charley claimed to have no reservations about sharing. When we proceeded to the treatment part of his session, it was literally like I was looking through a veil. I could feel the shifts in emotions, but all I could make out were shapes, colours, and blurry images, as anything I intuitively shared went through a filter first.

Charley's body bounced around, especially his legs. At one point, his left leg shot up, and when it came down, it almost took him right off the table. I had never before or since seen a reaction like Charley's during a Reiki treatment.

Charley was equally amazed by what had happened during his sessions. After, he appeared tired, was a little wobbly getting up, and had very little to say. He wanted to rebook as soon as possible. Usually I recommend two weeks, with the option of earlier if they need it. Charley wanted to go with the minimum and rebooked for four days later, my first available opening after the weekend. It wasn't until after he left that first appointment that I remembered I forgot to get him to sign the waiver.

On November 10, Charley arrived with a little more pep in his step. It helped that my room was "normal." No masks in a world where people were starting to obsess over germs. Our local council was discussing following other larger centres, and petitions were circulating to make masks mandatory in public places. In my space, I gave people the option to stay masked or unmasked, I myself never wore a mask.

Charley and I chatted a little about how he'd responded after his first treatment. As we talked, a feeling of calm swept over me.

It was a feeling I was very familiar with: wine. Did Charley have alcohol in his system?

When they said two weeks to flatten the curve, I was sentenced to homeschool, close my new business, and isolate. I medicated myself for those two weeks with alcohol and food, and fell down the TikTok rabbit hole. To get me through "flattening the curve," I also flattened my emotions.

Two weeks came and went, and it became obvious they weren't giving our freedom back. The rich were still skipping around the world; rules didn't apply to those with money. Alcohol and pot shops were open, but gyms, yoga, and the councillor my husband and I were going to became illegal to visit in person. I stopped cold turkey after two weeks and decided to become a law-breaking citizen.

For two weeks, time slipped by, and I didn't have a care in the world. I wish I could say I dropped my addictive behaviour, but I didn't until more recently. After the two weeks, I just supplemented one addiction for another.

> *When life gives you lemons, you can:*
> *1. Make a lemonade.*
> *2. Throw them back at life*
> *3. Ask, "What else have you got?"*

We all have a vice we fall back on when life throws us lemons. It's our crutch to prevent the bruise from the metaphoric citrus-fruit blow. We all have details of our life that we don't want to share, or in some cases don't realize it has become a form of self medication.

For two weeks, I used and abused multiple substances, but my go-to for most of my life has been food—in particular, sweets! To start, we use these substances to medicate, to turn life's lemons into metaphoric lemonade. But when life throws us lemons, we have a choice. We can stay doing exactly as we were, masking the taste of the bitter life we are living. Or we can choose to change and step away from what's making life bitter. All too often, we choose to stay and increase what we use to sweeten the circumstances.

The Universe wants to support you, and it will get louder. This is why your substance(s) of choice needs to increase. This is not a battle you will win.

You are here to grow. If needed, you are bound to have moments like I've experienced, like *WTF just happened*. All of a sudden, something comes out of left field and forces a course correct. This is the Universe, God, Source—whatever you want to call it—forcing you to change. No choice, because it's not just about you anymore. My gut says it's for humanity as a whole.

I knew if Charley chose to keep coming, he would eventually decide where change needed to occur. His body was screaming at him, and our exchanges helped him clear out excess energy that was holding him back.

Charley's second visit was very similar to his first: same foggy veil, same body convulsions as he tried to relax. I had a strong suspicion that Charley used alcohol to cope with life, which was the possible cause for the veil. When I have worked on a client who uses antidepressants or anxiety pharmaceuticals, I occasionally experience fog or blocks in intuitive shares. It wasn't for me to tell him stop drinking; a healer's job is to support and guide. My first goal was to get him to the point energetically where he would open up to me.

Once again, he left calm and tired. He rebooked again for three days later. Once again, moments after he left, I realized that I forgot to get Charley to sign a consent.

Setting up for Charley's third visit, I discovered there were no intake forms in my binder. Once again, on his arrival, we had a short chat on how much better he felt following his session. Charley's body shook around once again. This time he also saw a veil: red. As he said "Red," I also heard fear. It gave me a good lead into what I had been experiencing.

I brought up fears and asked what scared him.

"Snakes," he said.

Snakes symbolically, in many traditions, represent both masculine and feminine, creativity and transformation. Charley had just told me what was holding him back, and he didn't even know it. Was he really willing to share everything, or was he going to continue to hold back, blocking me?

Energy workers have the ability to snoop. I choose not to. It would be the equivalent of walking in on purpose when someone was getting out of the shower. I choose to wait until clients, friends, or even the random person on the street opens their heart before I read their energy. For Charley, I needed to get him to open his mouth and speak first. His verbal permission allowed him to trust our exchanges, and he became more willing to share with me as time went on.

During that third visit, there was a moment of clarity where I felt my dad's presence, I heard him laugh and say, "He is a gift." I knew Charley was okay with past lives, the visuals of energy moving, and figured he would be cool with dead people talking. However, I was lost for words as to why or how I could tell this forty-ish-year-old, recently single male that my dead dad directed him to my office as a gift. My lips stayed sealed. I made the goodbyes as normal as I could, and Charley rebooked for November 16, 2020.

Charley made it clear that he would be an open book from here on out. I needed to figure out how Charley was a gift. I learned that Charley, like me, had abandonment trauma. In particular, he had built walls around his heart toward women. He had chosen to close down the feminine energy within him, his intuition, which is a very strong force. This was the source of his imbalance.

Ironically, the universe, and my dad, felt that it would be a good fit to match Charley up with a feminine healer. I have had just as many moments where this makes me laugh as it does make my head spin.

The next three days until I saw Charley, my mind and body went crazy. When I would try to relax or sleep, my whole body vibrated. My mind was working overtime, and I kept revisiting what made Charley a *gift*. What was the reason? Once again it was about mirrors. So what was Charley mirroring in me?

At the time, I was struggling with a course I was taking in Ayurveda—a course that had quickly turned very structured and medical. I was required to fill out a thirty-page intake to get experience asking the "right" question. This made me question whether Ayurveda could be used in my sessions.

Up to this point, I still hadn't given Charley his one-page intake that I was currently using; how could I possibly ask clients to complete thirty? These thirty pages included some very personal information, stuff clients eventually share with me once the trust had been built. Charley was comfortable answering many of these questions verbally after just three visits.

Then it hit me: Charley was a gift from my dad, a case study where I could incorporate Ayurveda into my sessions. I never gave Charley the thirty-page intake. Instead, I printed off my usual one page, in addition to one page from my course: the doshic quiz. From there, I planned to begin offering Charley logical Ayurvedic lifestyle changes, to help him back into balance. First and foremost, we discussed the effects of alcohol on his body.

On November 16, a very happy Charley almost bounced into my room. I promptly asked him to fill out my intake, which included the basics: name, phone number, birthday, medical history, and medication, as well as confirmation that he realized I wasn't a doctor and that his participation was for relaxation and self-discovery. When he had completed it, he commented that yesterday was his birthday—"a gift."

Ironically, November 16 is my dad's birthday. Another gift? I needed to tell Charley now! He handed me the clipboard and, in a joking manner, I said, "Now that I have your personal information, you're going to regret giving it to a crazy lady." Charley laughed and clarified he knew I wasn't crazy.

When I discovered that Charley and my dad nearly shared a

birthday, it was just a start for me to understand why it was my room he walked into. For years, I struggled with my dad's death and why he died so young. Here before me was a man dying before his time, and I could see the path he was heading down.

Like my dad, Charley was raised in an environment where alcohol was normalized. They both experienced abandonment due to circumstances surrounding the mental health of a parent. Charley and my dad would do anything for anyone and felt it was their responsibility to self-sacrifice to help another. As a result of just dealing with the lemons life threw at them, Charley and my dad were both diagnosed with an autoimmune disease, and despite medical intervention, neither could get relief from the pain.

So like my dad, Charley heavily self-medicated with alcohol. On that particular day, November 16, I knew without a doubt that Charley was dependent on alcohol to survive. When I shared my dad's story, there were enough similarities between my dad and Charley that Charley could relate to my dad. I didn't have to say anything more. Charley connected the dots and admitted how much he drank and that he needed to stop.

The gift that keeps on giving! Dad had gifted me on his birthday a way of incorporating Ayurveda into my sessions. My knowledge was a gift to Charley—the support he needed emotionally to heal his lifestyle and trauma that my dad was unable to find. Throughout that fourth visit, I repeatedly felt my dad's smiles. I also recalled a moment of my mom telling me about a psychics' reading she had where Dad was helping lost boys from the other side.

Charley wanted a play-by-play of my dad—his life, interests, anything I was willing to offer up. When I said the name of the company my dad came to work for, Nowsco, Charley said his dad also worked for them a long time ago. He continued to tell me that his dad was having some memory impairments, probably from the years of drinking, and probably wouldn't remember my dad.

I wrote my dad's name on one of the Ayurveda information papers I was sending home. Unable to wait until he got home,

Charley called his dad, and within ten minutes of Charley leaving my room, I received an excited call that his dad remembered.

That evening, the conversation between Charley and his dad continued. He was sure his dad's mind was fading, but the stories went on for hours. Turns out Charley and I likely had spent a few company Christmas parties together, thirty-plus years ago. Dad had gifted Charley's dad, his former friend, with memories of the good old days with the boys in their youth. It was very obvious there was something greater than us that had pulled us together. Almost three years later, we are still learning from each other through mirrors.

We met regularly to start—twice a week. He was also working with a naturopath who successfully paved the way for Charley to get a stem cell transplant. To prepare for the procedure, Charley had to reduce his alcohol consumption. This furthered his awareness of his consumption and need for change.

I often develop friendships with clients, but there are strong boundaries to prevent my clients from draining my energy. Charley pushed these boundaries but never wore them down. Through Christmas, I started getting calls from Charley later in the evening. I kept it short, told him to get some fresh air and stay off social media, or tried to direct the conversation to what was going on in the world that was positive. I knew we would become friends, but first I needed him to vibrate closer to my level.

Meanwhile, Canada was getting ready for another lockdown, which triggered Charley to want more liquor, despite the reduction he knew he needed for the transplant to have maximum effect. Healing can be very uncomfortable, and unfortunately, we sometimes find ourselves going backwards before we start moving in the direction of positive change.

Charley started having terrible vertigo and digestive upset. Energetically, we were disturbing the balance he had established in life, and he wasn't digesting the change. I knew Charley needed more than what I had to offer. While Charley appeared to have faith in me alone to help him, I could tell the bottle was calling him back.

I am not perfect. I refer to myself as "perfectly imperfect." I accept my shortfalls and see that I, just like my clients, need help. By healing ourselves, we inspire others to do the same.

Emotions have always been clear for me, and suppressing them with addictions was a struggle. For someone who can't stop at just one cookie unless it's the last cookie, I realized I was not the healer to help Charley with his addictions. I have many healers I seek advice from: marriage councillors, personal councillors, massage therapists, chiropractors, energy workers, sound therapists, yoga teachers, kinesiologists, and even from time to time a physician. We all have different gifts, and I've learned that by listening to what my bodies say, I can determine which healer I need in the moment.

First, I encouraged Charley to look for a support group like AA. Unfortunately, he found that the majority of the people who attended were still drunk or withdrawing. Being highly sensitive to others' emotions, not only was he craving to suppress what he was feeling, he wanted to drink to suppress their feelings and associated cravings. Group meetings were a fail!

This was also around the time Canada shut down for a second time. Checking into rehab wasn't an option. Charley would need visitation from his father and dog; their wellbeing was his priority. So he knew he wouldn't be able to obey the COVID rules of the facility. My last suggestion included providing Charley with a couple of recommended addiction councillors. I found him two names recommended by a trusted family member in counselling. Both booked Charley and then cancelled within a week, triggering Charley's abandonment trauma once again.

I had to put my foot down and told Charley he could call me before but not after he had started drinking. His next appointment was postponed several times until there was no rebook scheduled. I know Charley is here for a really important purpose, but until he is ready to see it himself, all I can do is patiently wait.

*Life has its own wisdom. Who tries to help a butterfly to get
out of its cocoon, kills it. Who tries to help the seed to get
out of the sprout, destroys it. There are certain things that
have to happen from the inside out.—Ruben Alves*

My text messages were answered with short one-liner excuses as to his bad health. He kept pushing me off but didn't want me to go away. This is the hard part of my job: patience.

Meanwhile, my dad was working behind the scenes, cooking up his next intervention. I had to stepped back and allowed Charley to regress, going back to old girlfriends and binge drinking. Then, on February 21, Charley's dad had seen enough. An argument broke out between the two of them. They agreed to disagree on his choices and parted ways for the night.

In a moment of silence in which I can only guess he was asking for help to save his son, Charley's dad recalled a co-worker of his and my dad's. This co-worker had left Nowsco to pursue a career as an addictions councillor. Charley's dad returned to Charley with the story of the councillor and the connection working with Nowsco. I received a message that evening asking for an appointment as soon as possible.

Charley came in a couple of days later and gave me a full accounting of his last few weeks. He acknowledged his frustration with the failed support connections. However, the excitement of the councillor he was going to see on February 24 had pulled him out of the dark hole he had thrown himself into and put him back on his healing journey. The last time I saw my dad alive was February 21. He died February 24. Coincidence?

I do not believe in coincidences, or luck (good and bad). I believe that every part of our life is mapped out by our design. The surprise events we see as coincidences are the result of a greater force.

Charley established his own supportive group of healers with help from a higher source. His detox was rough, but he told me it would be the encouragement he needed not to drink again. His naturopath supported the detox physically, while his councillor and I offered him support energetically and emotionally. As weeks turned to months, Charley's sobriety strengthened, his health improved, and even the shaking during treatments stopped.

Summer was, as Premier Kenny promised, "Open for Summer." I was receiving phone calls again from Charley; these were his playful attempts to push the system. Motorbike rides, road trips to see friends—he was living rather than just staying alive.

Then, just as summer came to a close, the media flooded our senses with fear again: another wave of COVID and more restrictions. On October 21, 2021, Canada was making it mandatory for citizens to be vaccinated to travel. Less then a month later, on November 15, Alberta would take all public non-essential services away from its unvaccinated citizens. November 17, 2021, was the last session Charley booked with me for nearly six months. We continue to communicate and do coffee, and he continues to do check-ins. But our relationship has become more of a friendship, and any energy sessions are more for relaxation than to create life-dependant change.

Patience is the practice of remaining present—being still and observing how the future will unfold in its own time.

Chapter 22

MARY

Each of us is like a radio station, constantly broadcasting signals about ourself and our life ... The people and situations that match those signals are the ones that will tune in to us and be drawn to our experience.—Unknown

Early November 2021, Mary, an elderly lady, walked into my studio office. Doctors had discovered a lump in her left breast and suspected cancer, preforming a biopsy the same day. Mary was awaiting results. She had taken up to and including her Master Level in Reiki. She was a retired teacher, mother, grandmother, great-grandmother, and wife. She often called on her angels but needed help to get through her current crisis.

She was worried about her ability to make it through a surgery, if it was cancer, due to her reaction to anesthetic during previous surgeries. I could feel immediately that she was highly empathic and intuitive, but for some reason, she resisted sharing. Her throat was completely closed. Her homework that first visit was to sing. Singing is a fun way to open the throat, and as an extra bonus for Mary, it would exercise her lungs, preparing them for the pending surgery.

Music is an easy and fun form of energy therapy. For those who are embarrassed, I wouldn't recommend the discomfort of an audience. Rather, turn on some tunes and karaoke alone. Embrace your inner rock star and move like Jagger.

Mary needed to strengthen her diaphragm and improve her lung tissue quickly, and she loved the assignment. My hidden agenda was to remove the blocks of her throat so that we could explore what truths she had been disconnected from. It turned out she used to sing a lot, and she found every opportunity to exercise her lungs.

She was expecting the biopsy results in the coming days, and a week after we first met, Mary was back. She walked in smiling ear to ear and told me about singing outside the doors of Walmart while she waited for her ride. Reiki only works if you're willing to keep the energy flowing. Mary bounced in and said she hadn't felt so good in a long time.

The first few sessions, I listened to lots of stories about Mary's day-to-day happenings. I quickly learned that Mary was married, and she spoke of her husband with so much love. This little old lady still was so much in love and was planning what was left of her future with the love of her life. I wanted what Mary had; however, over the past few years, my husband and I had been moving apart. I was changing, and all I felt was his resistance.

I had learned some things about my husband that made his love toward me feel more material then authentic. I was on the fence as to whether to stay until the kids left home, or leave to create a more balanced home environment for my boys and me. Either way, Mary entered into my life when I needed to see what it looks like to have a supporting spouse.

Mary's third visit brought the news of her biopsy results, it was cancer! It's bittersweet when someone has a mortality wakeup. Their life flashes before their eyes: the good, the bad, and the ugly. At this session, Mary laid all her cards out on the table. I learned about her ex-husband and how she left after the kids left home. WTF!

*The truth has the power to destroy the illusion and
bring us back to reality. This is something many avoid
or deny in order to continue sleeping through life.*

As Mary told of her ex-husband's absences while the kids grew, the final straw that caused her to leave after the kids had grown up, I was speechless. Bill had been Mary's current partner, then husband, for only the last eight years. After those eight years, Mary was still so much in love with Bill. I suspect she continued to fight cancer just to save Bill the heartache of losing her.

Could I pull it together for another eight years until the kids left home, like Mary did? In my own marriage, I felt repressed, and the resentment was growing. I could not fill the wife roll I had once forced myself to fit into. Mary still loved her ex and even maintained a relationship with him and his partner until his death. Every story she relayed created a stronger connection between us. It was like looking into one of those magic mirrors and having my eighty-year-young self look back.

Mary had her mastectomy, making it a two-week space between our sessions, and I saw her again right before Christmas. While she was feeling much more optimistic about her own health, her attention now was on Bill's health. His heart was in early signs of failure, and his diabetes was more out of control than normal. For Christmas, she gifted her husband three session with me. However, due to his health restrictions, I took their treatments on location. I offered mobile and was invited into their home.

Their home was simple and welcoming. Plants and an assortment of collector mugs and semi-truck models filled pine shelves around the living room. A couple of wall hangings caught my eye. One was a print of an old town. It reminded me of what I hoped to bring Robsart back to. The other was a Cree prophecy written below a picture of a First Nation woman. Their house was filled with love. I could feel that he lived for her, and she for him.

I told them how the one print of the old buildings reminded

me of my plans to create a ghost-town wellness retreat in Robsart. Mary and Bill both were excited to tell me they knew exactly where Robsart was. Mary had even lived in the area in her youth. The Cree prophecy had been one of those serendipity things that kept showing up over the last month. It's what originally inspired me to write this book. On my last visit they gifted these to me as part of the downsizing they had to do to move.

Only a few weeks earlier, I had woken up before the sun to the sound of Karma barking. I was disgusted by the medical authorities and the rich elite who backed them creating free medical care, when in reality it was not a lot different from money laundering. They forced citizens to pay taxes, and they moved the money around, making purchase as they saw fit, including but not limited to making contracts for medical equipment purchases with ties to the same political parties that collected the taxes.

If anyone whispered information on natural or homeopathic medicine, it was immediately discredited—or, in my case, I became a repeat offender banned from Facebook. My guess is that big pharmaceutical companies aren't in the business of making people healthy. They just want to mask the problem so people don't feel their body screaming. They are in the business of making money. So before not too long, since the original problem wasn't resolved, something else will fall apart, requiring more tests and treatments, making more money for them.

> *Only after the last tree has been cut down,*
> *Only after the last river has been poisoned,*
> *Only after the last fish has been caught,*
> *Only then will you find*
> *that money cannot be eaten.*
> —*Cree Indian Prophecy*

I didn't share my thoughts with Mary and Bill, as they both made it very clear they thought highly of the science the government was showing citizens through the media they funded. What I did share was my desire to write a book, and the quote on the wall hanging summed up my thoughts. It turns out Mary was a publish author. She lent me a copy, a historic biography about a Polish prisoner of war. It wasn't a part of history I was aware of. An amazing read!

Over the next couple of weekly visits, I heard stories of their pub visits and getting a little tipsy. They kept each other young. I heard about how they met through an ad; both were looking for a partner, not a provider. Mary and her husband had had a rocky beginning in life but were succeeding in their final leg to find a relationship and keep the family together.

Mary returned to her sessions weekly in my office after mid-January. Despite still battling cancer, she continued to be more concerned about her husband's health than her own. I wanted Mary to write in her assignment journal. She was a writer at heart, and she needed to continue to get her fears—past, current, and for Bill's future—out. If she was concerned about having evidence, burn it. After the many clients I've had, I know we all have a little firebug itching to be released.

The next time Mary returned and I asked how it went, she responded, "I burnt a lot of shit," then laughed. I had tears in my eyes and was grateful the lights were low. This is exactly why I do what I do.

As time went on and the inflation from the COVID recession started to set in, Mary's concerns were divided between finances and health. Financially and emotionally, the elderly two needed each other. With the cancer still present, Mary was lucky to get accepted for a new treatment that was affordable. Since it was unknown how she would respond, they decided to relocate to a seniors complex. Not only would it be a financially better option if something happened to Mary, there would be help for her husband who was having a hard time getting around due to mounting foot and heart problems.

In mid-April, Bill had to have his foot surgically removed, which resulted in a stroke early on an early April morning. His death came a few days later. But he never left her side. Each session, I feel his presence, and he has given me activities for Mary to keep her looking toward a future.

Mary has been sleeping better these days. She gives credit to a sleep apnea machine. The important thing is she has been dreaming again (digesting emotions). Unfortunately she remembers nothing.

I'm a believer that the dreams we remember can be used to help us grow. Those blacked-out dreams are necessary to clear out the clutter that holds down our soul.

Chapter 23

DR. CHAD SILAS

There is an order to healing. You can't rush it, skip steps, or jump ahead. When it's time, the right constants will enter your life to add, subtract, multiply, or divide your world in order to accomplish a specific result.

It wasn't until I left the office of my chiropractor that I realized it was once again Dad's birthday, November 16, 2021. He was giving me another riddle to figure out; this time, it would take me a while.

I had been seeing Dr. Silas for over three years. Often, there would be small chat about the project I had started in Saskatchewan—originally a result of oversharing to explain why I was back getting another adjustment so soon. A bummed shoulder from excessive painting, or sudden onset of knee, hip, or neck pain I suspected was from a crappy sleep in the trailer.

On this seemingly ordinary visit, just as I was about to leave the room, he inquired about coming by my office to learn more about what I do. I awkwardly and enthusiastically agreed, and later that day, we set up a date and time via text.

A few days later, Dr. Silas and I met at my office. I talked about quantum physics and showed him a practice of using a pendulum over each of his chakras to show how energy flows through the body. As the crystal was repositioned over each chakra, its movement changed, and I would explain how the changes could potentially reflect potential blockages in his body emotionally, mentally, and even physically. I felt crazy and even commented about how this stuff can be a lot to absorb, since it goes beyond what science can prove. Many call it whoa-hoo, voodoo, or witchcraft.

I knew having this conversation with Dr. Silas was triggering some trauma switches within me. I felt crazy, but he just sat and listened to me rant. When I was done, he commented on how chiropractics isn't on even footing with the rest of the medical establishment, and he believes there is truth to this stuff. It took a couple of conversations and seeing him regularly over the past nine months in my yoga classes with his wife before Dr. Silas became just Chad.

> *In order for my relationship to change with men, I needed to have a better relationship with myself.*

I never pry into people's energy fields; I look for energy threads clients are willing to share. Chad is a textbook Taurus: passionate, driven, stubborn. I love the determination of a Taurus, but I'm confused by their ability to avoid anything emotional. With Chad, it was all business. So my hurdle and point of access was going to be figuring out how our professions fit together.

We got together at a local coffee shop, one that was willing to turn a blind eye to vaccine passports. At this point in Canada, it was illegal for me to enter a food establishment due to my refusal to get a COVID vaccination. I came armed with a few of my favourite books on energy stagnation and how it manifests into disease within the body. Books, I'd learned, were a subject in which we had a mutual interest.

Chad was experiencing a normal change of life. The modern world refers to it as *midlife*, and it is more common than one thinks. Movies portrayed the silver or balding man buying a car and getting a new wife twenty years his junior. It could be a turning of a particular age, a death or illness, something making us assess our life. What have we achieved and what do we want to accomplish and is there still time? How close are we to successfully meeting the goal we hoped to achieve in this lifetime, fulfilling our purpose? It triggers us to do something erratic, to jump-start ourselves or to fill a void we feel.

For me, it was yoga training and a gun licence when I had a kidney removed. I didn't know it then, but Chad recently had experienced the death of an immediate family member. Instead of a fast car and an affair, he become a partner in a clinic and purchased a dream home for his wife and himself.

Chad and I had a lot in common. We had both been married for a long time, to people who were very different than we were. Watching him and his wife in yoga reminded me a lot of the activities I used to do with Riley. Time together is more about being physically present, spending time together, not so much about sharing in the experience of the activity. I enjoyed watching as they worked together in class. I did see the eye rolls, the smiles, and yup, even a middle finger once.

Chad in so many ways, I have discovered, is a mirror to myself. This discovery almost a year after our initial tea has turned so many lights on.

Don't put people on pedestals. They're people and balance isn't their forte at the best of times. The minute you treat anyone else as more worthy than you, you are setting two people up for a fall.—Unknown

I tell my students I refuse to get up onto a pedestal. I am their equal and a guide to explore their intuition, energy, and potentially more. I have known for a while that I gain as much from my students and relationships as they have the potential to learn from me. While reading Rebecca Campbell's *Light Is the New Black*, it hit me what my next lesson was to learn from Chad. I put Chad on a pedestal! The *Dr.* credential on his name at work gives him a lot of credibility.

I was following societal expectations that he knew more than me, so perhaps I wasn't worthy to converse with.

His credentials intimidated me enough that I had created distance between myself and my teacher. I looked up to him as if he was some kind of celebrity due to his eight-ish years of education. I felt uncomfortable talking about energetics on account of his training. I saw in him, what I want to acquire myself: intelligence. Funny thing is, we connected over books—knowledge.

Chapter 24

DREAMS

Many of my dreams involve an old house in need of repair, with lots of hallways and rooms, which are always filled with old furniture and other junk. It has always been this way, even before my experiences with the abandoned buildings in Robsart. A couple of pieces always catch my eye. While I don't know their significance most times, I make note and keep moving forward. If I stop to think in a dream, I know I will wake up.

In this particular dream, the walls are covered in floral wallpaper and lots of thick trim coated in years of what is probably lead paint. I see, then pick up the top stool on a stack. It has black cast-iron legs, and the seat appears to be oak with black grain lines. I make a note that the chairs are homemade with love.

The room is big and smells as old as it looks. My boys are there, and they are curious and disgusted at the same time. This room's roofline lacks some headspace in the corners. It's an upper storey.

I walk over and look out the window, confirming the ground below, and I can see that the house is two houses that have been connected into one residence. The older boys are teasing my youngest that this is going to be his room and he has a roommate. It's haunted; we all can feel it.

I state "This will be my craft room" to stop the argument between the three of them.

We make our way to the other wing of the house. Its style is more the '40s, at least three to four decades newer. The rooms are big and empty. "This is going to be a lot of work," I say to myself, and "This is where I will begin the renovation."

I blink and the room is repainted, and laminate now covers the floor surface that was formerly dressed in worn-out beige carpet. This is Kade's room.

I hear a phone ring, and wake up. It's 8:51 a.m. Saturday morning.

When I came to this section of writing the book, I once again began to struggle. Full disclosure: I went and got a pint of Häagen-Dazs Chocolate Peanut Butter and cashed in a lotto ticket that I won two dollars on for a scratch ticket that I *will not* scratch until this book's first submission.

We all look for the happily-ever-after to our story. I have seen so many in my dreams, but rarely in dreams do I get the step-by-step on how to reach them. The morning Karma woke me to start writing, I once again could only see the end. I did not imagine the process to be so emotionally and mentally exhausting.

I always asked, "Why?"
My answer is, "Why not"

After I destroyed the whole pint of ice cream, I decided to call it a night and had the above dream. Upon waking, it felt right to have it make its way onto these pages. My dreams for the most part are viewed through my eyes. At my current age, monsters are usually people, because both my conscious and unconscious are aware that in this lifetime, dimension, and planet, these are the only beings I need to be cautious of.

I also have the ability to practice free will. I control my direction and decisions; other characters, not so much, just like life. It is hard sometimes to determine whether a dream is a dream, or is it a potential/possible reality? This kind of dreaming is referred to as *lucid dreaming*.

The conscious mind is masculine: rational and logical. It is created and governed by our upbringing and society's expectations, creating ego and fear. When we are asleep, the unconscious mind is in control. The unconscious is the intuitive/feminine voice within each and every person. It is untameable and unmanageable—the voice of your authentic self. It does have the opportunity to sneak in its two bits during the day, in those brief moments where we choose to listen to our heart over our head. But more often it is ignored, leading to discomfort.

In the dream state, our desires and fears play out like a movie, directing us toward the next step we need to take in order to reach our *dharma* (life purpose). I've learned not just with my dreams but with most people's that what we see in our dreams shouldn't be taken at face value. For example, everyone has at some point had a naked experience in a dream. Are you scared to show your natural true self? Is your logical mind telling you that nobody wants to see who you really are? Are you comfortable or uncomfortable in your skin? Are you feeling exposed?

Dream interpretation is not a logical process. There is no book that will explain your unconscious; you need to look at both who you really are and what is going on in your world at the time. So let's take a deeper look at the above dream.

What was going on at that moment in time? It is important to explore the day-to-day. Our unconscious and conscious mind are not two separate beings. They are two different perspectives: one from the mind, the other from the heart. So the day-to-day stressors are what the unconscious mind is trying to give direction too.

This year, it had been impossible to make my way back to Robsart. It had provided me refuge the last few years (during the pandemic). I literally could run away from my problems there. Riley doesn't like camping, making it the perfect place to run to to get away from our relationship strains.

Normally, I can head out late April for a visit. By the May long weekend, I am setting up the pool. Anytime after that, I can drag my boys out for a weekend camping trip. This year, however, it rained nonstop until the end of May. Through June, it rained on weekends. Then the week the boys were done with school, it rained for another week straight.

As soon as it stopped raining, we headed out. It was July 8. The grass was about three feet tall, and the pool was still in storage. I had planned to go Friday morning and stay until the following Tuesday. But just me and my youngest headed out; my husband planned to bring the other two out on the Saturday. They are at that age where they would rather not be out camping, so this year I opted for camping with them in moderation. That way, my happy place could stay happy.

> *Trying to control the future is about as successful as*
> *getting a teenager out of bed with a smile.*

It took me a full day to get the grass cut in the yard where we have the trailer. Saturday morning, I finished the yard and pulled the pool from the garage. To my disappointment, there was a huge mouse nest, an equally devastating hole, and five little grey babies. Why me? If I only would have come out sooner. Stupid mice!

I brushed off my frustration because a) Shit happens, and b) Shit happens because for some unknown reason, it is supposed too. I called Riley, who was still waiting for our teenagers to wake up, and arranged for him to bring a patch kit out later that day. Then I continued cutting the grass until Riley and four boys arrived around lunch. As part of my attempt to bribe my older two into coming, I'd had them each bring a friend.

It was an amazing day! The pool got filled with ice-cold well water, and I made burgers for supper. After supper, the older boys all left, leaving the youngest; my puppy, Luna; and me behind. Minutes after they left, Luna (a nine-month-old chi-weenie) climbed off my lap and collapsed behind my chair of heat exhaustion. My mommy instincts kicked in; we fired up the A/C in the trailer and got her cooled off and hydrated.

Since the next day was suppose to be another 30+ (degrees Celsius) day, we quickly packed up before dark and headed home, driving in front of a thunderstorm. Luna slept the whole way, and her crazy energy levels were fully recovered by the time we got home. I planned to go back soon, just me for a few nights when Riley was home. But one problem after another came up, keeping me home. So I just used the opportunity to keep writing.

Enough is enough! I'm going! August is always a busy time with getting kids ready for back-to-school and advertising fall-session classes with the business. I decided that August 5, after teaching my yoga class, I was heading out to Robsart. Only nope—my oldest son, Mr. Cautious, crashed his bike and broke his collarbone. For obvious reasons, I stayed home August 5. I teased Nathan that there were less painful ways to avoid Robsart, and we laughed at how once again I wasn't getting out there. The universe, just like you body, gets louder, until eventually the signs cannot be ignored.

Nathan and I talked a lot on August 5, which helped him realize and be grateful for what had happened. It sucks; however, at the time, we were having a constant battle getting the older two to wear helmets. I convinced Nathan to wear his about a week earlier by giving him the choice. I told him that his choice to wear or not to wear a helmet might lead to me having to make the choice to pull a plug.

His younger brother still felt invincible. He's a do-first-then-deal-with-the-consequences kind of person. Nathan agreed he had taken one for the team, and he was so glad he'd had his helmet on. Better yet, when Sean was asked the evening of August 5, without hesitation he responded that he would also be wearing his.

Since Nathan couldn't do anything, his girlfriend and family asked if I could drop him off with them at the family cabin. It was on the way to Robsart. Riley would be home in the evening, so I took all these as permission to go.

The morning of the sixth, Riley called to let me know he was no longer going to make it home before night. So I was adaptable and figured *Just the day then*. I dropped Nathan off by 10 a.m., backtracked twenty minutes to the highway, and then continued east, turned south, and drove through Maple Creek, Saskatchewan. I was about two minutes past the town and it was no longer in view from the back mirror when it hit me: "I don't have the keys!" No keys meant the trip was over. It was time to head home.

By this point, I'd lost track of how many times in one season I'd had to cancel plans. Since summer, my schedule had been almost empty. I'd had clients canceling, no-show new clients, classes postponed for a variety of reasons. I've got nonbelievers in univerals signs began to second-guess and question what was keeping me home. I just laughed (my default expression). Everything happens for a reason, I don't believe in coincidences, especially this many.

As is above, so is below. As is within, so is without. As the Universe, so the Soul.—Hermes Trismegistus

Working through a dream interpretation is like learning a new language—only the person in charge of running the dream most likely isn't very good at translation. The written and spoken word is very logical. Every object and action has little room for meaning deviation. We speak assuming everything is what it is.

Dreams are not logical, so applying logical definitions to what is witnessed will get a dream analyzer nowhere. A tree is a tree because we have named it so. We identify a tree by defining it to look a particular way and objectifying it, instead of recognizing it first and foremost as a life that gives us life. It is a home and/or food source for animals, fuel to cook and keep warm.

Have you ever looked closely at a tree, then an X-ray of a lung? This is a perfect example of the micro (human scale)–macro (earth) relationship. As within as without, the tree breathes in carbon dioxide and breathes out oxygen. The trees need us to breathe as much as we need them.

> *Tree of Life*
> *The tree of life symbol is commonly depicted as a large tree with roots that spread inward to the ground, and branches that spread outward to the sky. This represents the interconnected nature of all things in the universe; an eternal bonding of the physical realm we are rooted in and the spiritual realm we are reaching for. The tree serves as a reminder of our universal connection to the mother earth, and our dependence on her to grow and flourish. It is a reminder that everything in life is connected, we are all connected. We are rooted in family and ancestry. We will branch into personal growth, strength and beauty, and experience re-birth and new beginnings in the many seasons of our lives.*
> *Root down and rise up!—Unknown*

The dream and the details of the dream were more than just the boys and I exploring an old house. It is the irrational intuitive mind trying to get through by using the language my logical mind understands—recognizable images. In the dream, I was in an upper story of my favourite-time-period home, my "dream" home. *Dream home* symbolically is where we feel safe, secure, and valued. The reduced roofline could be symbolic of something preventing me from having that full safety, security, and value that would put my mind (headroom) at ease. It could also be my intuitive mind calling out. Am I reaching my full potential, or am I limiting myself as to how high of a goal I am capable of achieving?

Every detail that I allowed my attention to be drawn to, when examined on an emotional level, reminds me of an aspect of my day-to-day I am currently not acknowledging. Consider the stacking stools coming together with love, for example. Over the last few months, I have separated myself from my support team.

Looking out the window, I saw something I didn't expect, symbolically showing me that looking from a different perspective will help me discover something pleasant I didn't expect. As I followed the halls (path/life), watching the décor, I just kept placing one foot in front of the other, moving forward.

The transition in the house went from older to newer (improvement/change). I noted the improvement and commented, "There is still work to be done." My comment is a common feeling I have regularly in my day-to-day goals as well as my personal life. I am a visionary. I know this, and people around me have often pointed it out. I, like my dreams, never see the end result. More karma I inherited from my dad.

I dream of old houses, and something I've always wanted to do was fix an old building. Robsart helped me create a vision bigger than just a house—a vision my parents once had, and my grandfather and great-grandfather before them. With each generation, the vision of Robsart as a thriving community was never completed.

Perhaps I have done all that I was meant to do there. Maybe I'm done, and Robsart was just a pit stop to learn some lessons. Maybe I am destined to create a thriving wellness community. For now, I need to just place one foot in front of the other and see where the hall takes me.

Failure to acknowledge dreams is failing to plan.

So many unfinished projects! Even in my dreams, I cannot finish a project. But in the dream, I felt a sense of accomplishment that Kade's room was done. I was excited to see and renovate the other rooms, but then I was brought back to reality. I woke knowing I am the queen of procrastination and unfinished projects.

Robsart has become my escape from responsibility. For now, the project is on pause because it's become obvious I have something else I'm meant to accomplish. All signs, day and night, are bringing awareness to the fact that I have procrastinated long enough. That once again my project, this book, needs to be completed. Until then, there is no replacing it with the next shiny object that catches my attention. I will not retire it to the craft drawer to be completed one day, because that day is now.

My ability to dream has been a greater gift than any amount of knowledge a school could teach me.

Chapter 25

A SIGNER SIGN

*It's never the people who follow the masses
that make it into history books.*

While most of the time, the squirrel in my mind runs a million miles a minute, when I came to this section, the squirrel laid down and played dead. I had so much to say, and no clue what direction to take. When there is no direction and frustration sets in, that means it's time for a break.

Yesterday, while I was sitting and staring at the above title and the sentence below it, my youngest, Kade, walk out on the deck where I was pretending to work. The conversation started like this:

"Mom, I was just thinking, you know the question 'What came first, the chicken or the egg?' Well, I had this totally random thought: 'What came first, the colour orange or the fruit?'"

I shut down my laptop and took part in an interesting conversation for maybe ten minutes as we debunked each other's opinions. It was all in fun, and both of us knew there was no "right" answer. Kids don't judge their intuition. It is us, their parents, who initially quiet them by chasing them away, or more recently by tuning them out while we stare at a screen. We make them turn off their intuition by making them believe they have nothing to say of value.

It was pointless to pretend to type when the conversation with Kade brought me much more joy. The day went on, and the frustration of knowing I would not be getting this book done by Friday bugged me. I really wanted to get to Robsart.

That evening, I drove down to the studio to teach a Nidra class. As I walked in, I noticed the store owner had placed a new book on the shelf: *Signs: The Secret Language of the Universe* by Laura Lynne Jackson. Funny—exactly what the Signer Sign refers too. So I grabbed it and placed it by the till. Once the room was set up, I flipped to the contents to get a more detailed look at the book while I waited for my students: *Chapter 1: Oranges*

Sold! The book came home with me. I read it while I soaked under the August 11, 2022, full moon, and it was the thing I was drawn to when I woke up the next morning. So many of the stories I could relate to. I even was brought to tears as I recalled similar experiences where I had doubted the experience's significance.

At 8:11 a.m., the first message from my tribe came in. I completed reading chapter 8 and closed my book to message my tribe about this amazing book. Then I realized my long-winded explanation was what I should be putting into *my* book. The block was gone.

I chased my animals back in the house, grabbed my blanket and book, and walked in to have a shower. Just as my feet hit the linoleum, another one of my tribe members called. I told her everything, and we laughed!

Signer Sign is the name of my tribe's Messenger group chat. It's not just nice to have my close group of women to grow with; I believe it is necessary for people to find a tribe to keep them growing. Your tribe members are there to offer a shoulder to cry on or a kick to the ass when needed. No judgment, no direction, just support and encouragement. Sometimes the members come and go through a revolving door. But there is a hub that stays connected. From the group, it only takes one person to shine a light, to create a revolution.

I do have some very close friends outside this circle as well, but these women are not shy about their passion toward the weird and unexplainable. It started with the coming together of three at an Intro Energy class. We came from an assortment of career, and faith backgrounds but had a common goal to help people. During the pandemic, we communicated daily through a group chat. Morning plans and evening reflections included good, bad, and ugly happenings, as well as memes or jokes that made us laugh.

But the most common theme was that despite knowing and seeing the signs from cards, God, Universe, Angels, Spirit Guides, deceased loved ones, we were all still looking for more confirmation before we were willing to commit to a path/idea. Hence the name *Signer Sign*.

I started my business in March 2018 with Reiki and yoga class contracts with a local yoga studio and separate gym. By the fall of 2019, I had outgrown my current location, so my Reiki space moved from upstairs at the yoga studio to a holistic business located more in the city centre, and then again, a year later, to a larger room within the same business. I expanded into Reiki and intuition-based group classes. My tribe continues to provide me with the push to stay on track and set my next goal.

> *You let one ant stand up to us, and they all might stand up! Those 'puny little ants' outnumber us a hundred to one. And if we ever let them figure that out … THERE GOES OUR WAY OF LIFE! It's not about the food. It's about keeping those ants in line.*—A Bug's Life (1998)

Energy work has, in history, been a field largely dominated by women, but it doesn't need to be. Healers come in all kinds of nationalities, genders, ages, and religious and spiritual backgrounds. It is by working through our individual trauma that we can come together despite our differences. What makes a healing circle powerful is the unconditional love from within oneself that pulls the group together.

Since the start of the Christian Era, those in power have gone to extremes to persecute, punish, even exterminate people with the ability use or see energy. As early as 319 AD, laws were being put in place that restricted people known to use "magic" with a punishment of death if convicted. Over the centuries, laws and persecution oscillated depending on the rules of the time. The intensity, however, of witch hunts continued to increase over the long term, resulting in mass hysteria and murder.

In *Witches, Midwives, and Nurses* by Barbara Ehrenreich and Deirdre English, the authors state that an estimated 1 million people have been executed for witchcraft; however, the actually number has never been calculated. It is and continues to be the role of state, church, and medical organizations to provide the evidence and the resulting direction for the population. Entire villages were accused of witchcraft, leading to their excommunication, like the Spanish village of Trazmoz in 1511. Others held mass trials and persecution, leaving every woman and some of their male supporters exterminated.

It is believed by many that witch persecution peaked in Salem, Massachusetts. Salem's most famous trial, held in 1692, saw nineteen women executed. After three centuries, in May 2022, a "witch" from one of Salem's trials was officially pardoned and cleared of all charges. The state, church, and medical community turned the people against each other. Innocent people like Elizabeth Johnson confessed to making deals with evil, when in reality, all they were doing was helping people with substances like plant medicine and love. With the stroke of a pen, they were convicted and often executed, and now, just as easily, those in authority are making history go away.

Being irreplaceable comes from showing the uniqueness of my soul. Nobody else can fill the hole in this universe that Crystal Warberg has created as well as Crystal Warberg can.

Science has shown that people need people. The effects of mandated isolation and social distancing, rebranded "physical distancing" after it became obvious to many what the government was doing, have shown to be detrimental. Prior to the March 2020 lockdown, I knew that suicides and economic unrest were going to happen if people complied, so was very vocal. I lost friends, even family, because I stood up for what was about to happen, not just in Canada but worldwide.

Keyboard warriors stalked me and threatened me and my kids, telling me I needed to just shut up and fall in line. I fell briefly down the TikTok rabbit hole, as well as day-drinking while homeschooling. But I snapped out of it after a two-week pity party, because that is what we were supposed to do. "Two weeks to flatten the curve." The curve never flattened, and the numbers kept going up. However, hospitalization and deaths were minimal and contained to elderly and compromised individuals.

No money was invested to improve hospital capacity. In fact, all over Canada, health care facilities were shutting down and laying off employees. People were being sent home with no gyms, no therapy, but liquor stores and pot shops were open for business. I fell into their trap, and after two weeks, I saw through their fictional mountain (curve).

It's never logic or reason that changes the world. It's the crazy people and their out-of-the-box crazy ideas that make change happen.

I learned that persistence pays off. I have witnessed so many people start to see not only the narrative the government, church, and medical association are telling but the signs of what's to come, both happy and sad. First, they targeted women. They shut down schools and put mothers back in the homes and away from their people, their tribes (covens). They isolated our wise elders, those who knew and some who even lived history—our seniors. Easy feat to complete, since most people throw their grandparents and aging relatives into homes that were closed to outsiders. Many had no room companions and were completely isolated, with nothing to look forward or connect with but their end.

Then they gave medical employees, the people who many see as godlike, unlimited powers. Although wise with knowledge, they were conditioned to believe what "the book" says is truth—the book created by the medical association (partnered with the government).

Then they went after groups: churches, families, colonies, reservations. Urban residents have become so dependent on their governing bodies, there was minimal resistance, in relation to population percentage, against the mandates. Whereas rural people, more connected with the earth, have been capable of continuing to thrive and not follow. While I live in a small urban location, my heart is connected to the prairies.

Most just did as they were told. I have learned through these past three years that I'm not like most. I'm meant to stir the metaphoric pot. Rules are only recommendations. I'm here to live a full life, not necessarily a long life.

Chapter 26

GROW WITH ME, RILEY

I think people choose to leave a relationship for one of many reasons. If I choose to leave, it isn't about wanting to leave; rather, I couldn't stay and maintain my sense of self.

My mom jokes about my wall of dead soldiers: the collection of roses I hung on my wall as a teenager, each bouquet symbolizing a relationship that never grew but perished. On our first Valentine's, Riley gave me a collection of plants in a basket, one of which was a little tree. It was a sad little stick with small leaves poking up among a huge basket full of assortment ivies.

The stick grew as the years passed, and the beautiful clutter around the tree's base disappeared. New branches would grow, some would die, changing the trees directions over and over through the years. A few times the tree outgrew its pot, and I'd carefully select a new home for it to spread its roots.

The little tree I received roughly twenty-five years ago, from a skinny young blond boy, grew. Sure, it's changed. All the flashy extras have vanished. It has a fuller body, making it much stronger now. It's been an adventure! My little tree, like my relationship with Riley, if not nourished, will eventually die.

> *What is a soulmate? Friends, family members,*
> *lovers … soulmates are any relationships where each*
> *other's growth is dependant on the other's success.*

There are so many descriptions/definitions of a soulmate. For some, it's like a fairy tale, and after years of looking for each other, they lived happily ever after. What I've observed with this scenario is that people tend to change partners every time there is conflict. This ideal of a soulmate eventually becomes equivalent to checkmate: game over. Nothing learned, these supposed soulmates just move on to their next soul connection, only to repeat the same story.

In my forty-three years, I have lost track of my soulmate count. However, I have only been in two relationships where I would say I was in love. And only one resulted in a partnership of twenty-five years, nineteen years married. In this time, I have experienced every emotion imaginable. We have gone through a lot, and from our battles, we have learn more about ourselves, each other, and people in general.

For me, a soulmate is a person I have a soul contract with. I absolutely feel those butterflies, that electric attraction when I meet a soulmate. For me, I can love more than just one gender; it's not sexual. Sexual attraction needs to be earned. It's not only physical, it must be emotional and mental. From my experience, I suspect this is why so many married couples' sex life decreases. I know this is what happened with mine.

I am a serial monogamist. I do celebrate and honour the vows two people make between each other. However, the promise to stay together "until death do us part" needs to be evaluated. It is read and interpreted as death of the physical body.

Some people are in my life for a conversation; others I've known since I was child. The charge fluctuates over time. Sometimes it's been high and I want to be around this person all the time. Other ~es, the intensity is almost absent, and I've gone months with versing. When that electric attraction is gone, the contract

I do believe that if you get a good teacher, it may be worth exploring a follow-up contract. The beautiful thing about being a human is our free will. We can choose to walk away, or if we want to maintain a relationship, we can continue to pursue one. The type of relationship may change. It doesn't have to be all or nothing.

For a relationship to remain compatible, both partners need to communicate, but never compromise their dreams. Rather, they must learn to quiet ego and see how their dreams can fit together. True partnership comes from building a future together better than one person can do alone.

Whether it be the physical, mental, emotional, breath, or bliss body, we grow from the discomfort created. When you cross your edge and push through discomfort into pain, the result is trauma, not growth. Too much trauma can debilitate a person, incapacitating them for the rest of their life. Long-term exposure can create pain to just live.

This comes in the form of anxiety and depression. Those two little demons are your intuition screaming at you, with evidence that something in your life needs to change. I am getting better at recognizing rather then repeating. I've already been *there*, and *here* is where it's headed. Fear of unknown change creates anxiety but I no longer let it keep me stuck.

I have been riding this rollercoaster with Riley long before the summer of 2017. Instead of seeing change with my relationship with his mother, he has fallen in line with sweeping poor behaviour under the rug. Now just being around his family makes me zone or freak out.

One Western term more recently expanded into the dysfunction of relationships is PTSD. With PTSD, a person is being triggered by something in the present that puts them back to past events. I can forgive, but never will I forget. Forgetting allows the cycle to continue. Healing is not forgetting; it is recognizing how a specific event makes one feel. Instead, one must learn from the feelings of the cycle to decide what needs to stay or leave.

No relationship is all sunshine. But two can share one umbrella and weather the storm together.—Unknown

Over the years, there have been situations that Riley and I have worked and grown through. We were put in situations where it felt like the world was against us, and I trusted that Riley was a good man and would never do the things he was accused of. To this day, I believe he is innocent, because he never would have put me in those positions where I would have to defend him, lose friends, or suffer some of the physical ailments that resulted. I learned a lot from those events, got stronger, and moved forward.

Five years ago, I put up some pretty big boundaries around family—both his and mine. It was something I had to do to improve my health and save our marriage. I knew the new restrictions I had created allowed me and my children to grow spiritually. COVID led to additional boundaries, and some took these personally.

As I've mentioned before, as long as boundaries are set with the intent of love, there should be no regrets. I cannot control how a person interprets the boundaries. While I was okay with some of my family members cutting me out of their life, my hope is it is just temporary. I sure miss my sister and nephews.

Riley has a hard time setting as well as holding boundaries. He continues to subject himself not only to a lifetime of negativity and judgment but to additional criticism due to my choices against COVID mandates. I am being painted as uncaring, and my mothering is once again being challenged. Family congratulating one child for being a "good boy" for following the rules within earshot of another who is not wearing a mask—does that not automatically imply the other is bad?

The truth was, Nathan just wore his mask out Christmas shopping because he is a typical teenager embarrassed to be shopping with his dad and brother. Nothing to do with mandates. I support my kids in their choices. This is how they learn. Since that day, neither Nathan nor Riley has worn a mask in public.

Riley's family attempted to plan gatherings when I was at work because that way the "family" could get together safely. I had the pleasure of seeing the text when my broken husband had to play devil's advocate and stand up for me. For twenty-five years, Riley has continually defended me while appeasing his parents. I have encouraged and even instructed Riley to seek council to help him find boundaries, because it pains me to see him hurt, but I will not change to make his family happy again.

My home is a safe place, and I have created boundaries to keep the negativity out. If Riley doesn't have the strength to build walls, then I will continue to build more. Repeated forgiveness without change is a vicious cycle that prevents growth. Building resentment will eventually lead to death in our relationship. It has taken me a quarter of a century to realize that walking away from a relationship, even one with a soulmate, may be the lesson I was destined to live through and learn from.

I believe in the magic of chaos. I crave freedom and seek growth. I do not wish to belong to anyone but will lend a piece of my heart to everyone. Hold my hand and run beside me. I cut my coattails long ago so that nobody holds me back or takes a free ride.

In the spring of 2021, Riley and I took a break. I asked him to leave because it had become very apparent that our home was different when he was around versus when he was gone to work. He bounced around between friends and relatives' homes, but after just about a month, he accidentally fell asleep on the couch during a visit. Before not too long, he fell asleep in our bed while cuddling with the dogs.

> *Those who do not learn from history are doomed to repeat it.*—George Santayana (1905)

History has shown the lengths to which those in charge will go to have their way, and it was fear not force that got the job done. Witch trials led to family and friends turning in female wisdom-keepers for practicing healing arts. Church and state claimed they were in partnership with the devil.

In Germany, citizens turned in their Jewish neighbours, or their Jewish-sympathizing neighbours. I have discovered a few time in our past, not just Nazi Germany, where citizens enrolled in the military and willingly loaded citizens into train cars like cattle headed to slaughter. Germans did it to Jews, Russians to the Polish. Fearful of being on the other side, they willingly persecuted innocent people who were different.

In Canada, hundreds of children's bodies were recently found in unmarked graves behind residential schools. Government employees (RCMP) tore them away from their families and handed them to churches with minimal life staples. Everything cycles: days, seasons, years, history. History cycles until we learn and change the pattern.

We are in the same storm, but not the same boat.—Unknown

I begged Riley not to get the shot. Then, when his blood pressure started to rise from the stress of potentially being pulled out of service, I asked him to entertain the idea of getting one shot the day before they pulled him, then wait until they did pull him, take two weeks' holiday, then take the second. He said he didn't want it, but due to the outside pressure of friends, family, and work, he surrendered to expectations.

I know this is part of his journey, and still it confuses me why of all the choices he had, he chose that one. I have never been one for ultimatums or threats. I didn't spread fear, just information. Most of my posts that ended friendships or resulted in blockings on social media were historical similarities, creating future predictions and pointing out the contradictions in the science "fact."

I never told my husband and kids the vaccine could disable or kill them. But considering the accuracy of my predictions, some of the vaccines scare me—some, not all. I stated it wasn't tested and gave examples of history where medical treatments had collateral damage from poor testing. I also pointed out to Riley that we generally don't get sick, and when we do, the treatment is to stay home and rest so we don't infect others. It's because of how we live our life through balance that we keep our immunity strong. Our bodies are designed to heal themselves if given the right tools.

Instead of threatening Riley, I tried to come up with alternatives, like buying as much time as we could between doses or offering ways we could cut back on spending in case he was pulled out of service. His friends and family didn't offer the same tactics. They pushed fear, even going as far as pointing out that if I was the one who got COVID and was put in hospital due to being unvaccinated, they would incubate a vaccinated person over me because of my kidney health history. Fear: it can motivate or debilitate.

Mid-September, after a short tearful conversation with me, Riley got in on a walk-in appointment for his first Pfizer shot. I went with to try to show my support but cried the whole time. When he got in the truck and joked about the possible ways he could spend the hundred-dollar incentive the government offered, I felt my heart close.

Caution: The next paragraph is very graphic and pertains to women's health, so you may choose to skip.

Over the next month, lots of people were getting their second, some even their third dose. I started to notice a pattern in the energetic of being around people and in my menstrual cycles. Since my journey into health, my cycles had been like clockwork. I got an app on my phone back in 2012 just so I could plan and not be caught off guard. I have zero symptoms before I bleed. On my 29th day, I bleed for three days, the first day being the only day of active flow (red).

After Riley's first vaccination, my first bleed was horrible! I passed large clots and had cramps so bad I had to cancel teaching. Instead of three days, it felt as if I haemorrhaged for a full week before things started to slow down. It took almost two weeks for everything to stop.

I made an appointment to talk with a local doctor who believed in a side effect of the vaccine called *shedding*. I also tried to talk Riley into doing the doctor's protocol, but he wasn't sold on the idea, which was going to cost him money out-of-pocket. We can't make people do anything, so I decided to start a cleansing protocol to heal *my* body. I continued to work on my health—which, looking back, just encouraged me to grow further from Riley. He booked his second vaccination for October 29, just prior to his holidays and hunting trip.

October 29 was coming fast, and I had almost completed my twenty-one-day cleanse. As part of the cleanse, I decided to include a photo journal using the foot detox bath. It created a visual record of the toxins that were built up in my body and how the cleanse was removing them. Each time, the water got clearer.

The last day—Thursday, October 28—I saw something different. There were red blotches in the water, which indicate micro blood clots. I decided I needed to amp up the cleanse, so I ran to the doctor I had seen to start his herbal vaccine-exposure protocol. When I got home, I told Riley about my discovery in the foot soak and nervously told him I'd decided to do the herbal protocol and had spent $250. I begged him to hold off on the shot and do the protocol too.

By this time, it had been over a year since Riley and I had been intimate; not so much as a passionate kiss had been exchanged. An underlying fear that I did not share with Riley was how this vaccine could impact intimacy between us permanently because of my fears. The body is a temple, and what you put into it does affect it. This includes other people.

My temple is my body. My world around me my altar. My words are spells. Every thought an intention. My actions rituals, too manifest all that will be. I am sacred, I am divine.—Ara Campbell

COVID didn't break my marriage or stopped intimacy between Riley and me. Intimacy had stopped long before because energetically, I did not feel supported in being my authentic self with Riley. I don't expect him to be my cheerleader for every one of my crazy ideas, but to hold my hand. Let's work through this, and please don't try to change me.

I respected and supported Riley's fear of protests going violent. I wasn't willing to hide at home like I was being told to by government and society. But I compromised and did drive-by horn honking, with signs to support those standing the line until I knew it was safe. Then I stood beside them.

When protest tension started to grow and violence started to appear, I returned to drive-by despite my desire to stand strong. When I would share my fears of the vaccine, I felt unheard. I tried to tell Riley about studies I read in my Ayurveda course on Fauci and his knowledge of autoimmune and AIDS—how Fauci, among other rich elites and government members, was being investigated for crimes against humanity.

I begged Riley to wait based on my fears and research until the new vaccine technology had been properly tested. I had fears of it making him sick and possibly me through intercourse. Instead of hearing my fears, all he heard was me saying he was diseased and I would not have sex again. He made my fears about him.

I found out Riley had gotten the second shot ahead of schedule, the day before the micro clots appeared in the foot detox. Riley rushed out and got the detox supplements, which were a lot more than mine. He had put what I think is poison directly into his body. Since then, I feel he has become a very angry person.

There are many scenarios throughout our time together where I would talk about my plans, dreams, and goals, and Riley would put them to a dead stop. A lot of times, it wasn't a solid *no*. Usually, it was a sequence of excuses, like *When we have the money*, or *Right now isn't the time*. Surprisingly, we always had money for things he wanted.

I felt that as a wife, I was expected to drop everything because he made us plans. When I disagreed, I was met with puppy eyes or a cold shoulder. I wasn't looking for financial backing for my dreams. I felt if I could show Riley that my dreams had a financial dollar value, he might take me more seriously.

I don't feel my purpose is to have a studio, a store, or a clinic, though I'm not opposed if this is where I go. My dream is to be part of something bigger and help move humanity forward. I want to show people how to take back control of what's right for them instead of listening to the so-called professionals who govern society and the economy.

Professionals should be guides, not gods. Right now, my business pays for itself and then some. This is all I have asked for, and I am being provided with what I need. But as my vision becomes clearer, I see more support is required—not just financial, but mental and emotional. Can Riley show up the way I need him to?

November 2021, it was strike two, and he left on my request. Once again, instead of taking some time to reflect, he waited me out, bouncing from couch to spare bedrooms of family and friends until he found an opportunity to come home a second time before any growth had occurred. While Riley never used his short time away to reflect, I did. I knew that we needed time apart because of the codependency that existed between us.

So I started looking at houses for sale and pricing out rentals. Due to inflation and the job losses resulting from COVID shutdowns, people were turning in their mortgages, and rental prices had skyrocketed. For a four-bedroom rental, so that the boys could maintain their own rooms, I was looking at $1,600 to $2,400 a month, plus matched damage deposit, utilities, and a lease agreement for one year, plus no animals. A steep fee to pull together on a whim.

Riley would pay up. I didn't want to go to court and fight him. I continued to encourage Riley to do supper with the family and visit the boys and dogs. I did care for him, just didn't want to live with him. But quicker than the first time, Riley found himself getting comfortable on the couch, and before too long, back in our bed.

I though maybe I could make do. At this time, my boys had lost a lot from government mandates. They could no longer swim because two of the boys were over twelve, and vaccinations were required at most competitions. They couldn't see movies at theatres or eat out at restaurants with friends unless they subjected themselves to a nasal swab. They were experiencing segregation and discrimination by their peers thanks to the rules that medical and government leaders had made.

Mom guilt was setting in, so we openly discussed what they would want in regards to mandates. As promised, it was just temporary. Staying with Riley meant I would have to make sacrifices for maybe eight years to ensure the kids had both parents full-time. My new plan was to leave after it was just me. That's when Mary and Chad walked in and showed me my potential futures.

While the boys and I became second-class citizens through Christmas 2021, Riley continued to live life uninterrupted. Canadian Pacific Rail had instituted a vaccine mandate, but the date came and went, with nobody pulled from service. I knew it was coming. I also knew it wouldn't last forever. However, so many in the world continued to fall to the fear. Fear from the virus was dissolving, but fear of loss of livelihood and freedoms was growing.

Division soared as media and politicians pushed, "If more people vaccinated, we could return to a new normal." Even the councillors we were seeing required vaccination passports. In response, it felt like even Riley was starting to pressure me to do what was being requested. No vaccine meant no dates away from kids, and no councillor to discuss our problems.

We made it through Christmas, barely. In January, after a disagreement, Riley refused to leave. The councillor often referred to the straw that broke the camel's back, pertaining to the argument that led to us to come to see her. This was no straw. The metaphoric camel had died.

We all develop patterns of behaviour we learn from our parents. Since I have kids, I try to look at everything I am about to do before

I react. I remember saying to myself the first time Nathan crawled over to the TV and hit it with a toy, *If you can't stop spanking after three, don't spank at all.* Because then it's not about teaching, it's punishing, and self-satisfaction for my frustration.

Spanking was normal in my childhood, and not just our household—it was a generational thing. My boys, on the other hand, spent a lot of time chilling in their cribs or locked in their room while I pulled my shit together and calmed down. As they have gotten older, they will walk away from me, go to their room, and process the situation. Sometimes they come up and we talk; other times, they come up and apologize. Through my adventures of raising the boys, they have taught me so much about compassion and communication.

Riley, on the other hand, struggles with trying different parenting techniques. He has even commented about my "willy-nilly" ways. I'm okay with willy-nilly if it means that my boys will come to me when they have a problem. I have continued to grow and try to maintain a positive environment for my kids. They are my number-one goal moving forward.

> *When we heal ourselves, we heal the next generation that follows. Pain is passed through the family line until someone is ready to feel it, heal it, and let go.*—Unknown

I needed to exhaust all avenues. We had done over five years of counselling together, usually as a reactive treatment, not proactive. I love the lady we go to. It's like having a friend I can tell why I hurt, and it's met with questions, no judgment. She has helped me see different perspectives of the scenarios.

But it had been five years of regularly retelling the same problems over and over, with no change. It was hard to create boundaries within our house with Riley. He is a good dad, and I want him to be around. He is my best friend. When he pisses me off, he's the one I want to run to and say that my husband is being a complete ass-hat and needs to go away. What I wanted each time I told him to leave was separation, so that Riley would have quiet time to realized the amazing family and life he has.

I have met so many people who feel like they have let their careers and collection of material items rob them from the opportunity of a family. Instead, each time Riley would hurt the kids and I, his behaviour was much like that of a dog. His metaphoric tail went between his legs, and he waited me out until it was safe to come out again. Then he'd smother us with affection and sometimes gifts. Pleasantries, but no change occurs. Both of us know it is only a matter of time and he'll be back in the doghouse.

We are both being affected by this ugly cycle. I can feel the resentment toward him in my body grow. This is not the growth I desire. I don't feel I am an equal partner in this marriage; rather, I am an object without dreams and goals of my own. I talk but am unheard, so now I write as my final attempt to have him see the hurt I feel.

I can also see how this cycle has made him scared—in particular, of me leaving. Both love and fear can motivate. Right now, it feels like Riley is letting his fear govern his next move.

Chapter 27

THE TOWER

Opposites tend to attract, which is challenging, but it's from challenge that we do the most growth. It offers a different perspective and opinion on how to tackle life.

I am your typical dreamy Pisces, while Riley is a textbook stubborn Capricorn. He grounds me, keeping my head out of the clouds, and I attempt to keep him moving and life interesting. After having the kids and surrendering my career, I lost my independence. My life was shaped by my boys' needs. Riley found his career and friends, which occupied his time because I was too busy being a mom.

As time went on and the boys grew, I filled the extra time with my stuff: yoga, side hustles to make some cash, new friends, courses, exercise, books. Little by little, I reconnected with the girl I once was. But this was essentially a life independent of Riley.

It didn't happen overnight. The journey was a series of moments that led from one to another until it finally came to a point where I was ready to let Riley go. I had hoped Riley would see what I saw, but he continued to believe that as long as there wasn't active conflict, we were getting better. It felt as if he was just waiting me out.

I talked to him about my feelings, many times, but it always ended with his tears and apologies with no action plan. It's hard to grow when your partner is content in the hamster wheel he lives on, working a job he is scared he'll get another suspension from, or a job that leaves him hanging as to whether they will pay him in the future. His bitterness toward his family wakes him from sleep, as he fights verbally with them where I can hear.

I started writing to reflect on all the stories I kept repeating at counselling sessions. I started to see the patterns and cycles. I filled in some metaphoric blanks in my life, which led me to here.

In late spring, I decided not to go on a business trip to Victoria with Riley. About a week before he left, he put me on the spot about my unwillingness to be affectionate. It felt like he was blaming me for the failure of things to improve. I suppressed my rage and walked away.

The next morning, I called two law firms. One was more interested in the equity of the house, so I cancelled that appointment after I slept on it. I had no intention to threaten or make things ugly; I didn't even intend to take what I was told I was entitled to. I decided when I left it would be because it was the right time, and Riley would see it my way.

A calm mind leads to clear choices. I have watched the tower crumble, and now it's time to rebuild. How Riley fits into my life is undetermined, but with a steady foundation versus an earthquake of emotion, I intend to have Riley as lifelong friend, even if not in the same home.

> *Our greatest glory is not in never falling, but in*
> *rising every time we fall.—Confucius*

For me, a soulmate is your perfect fit for a season, a reason, or forever. We all want forever, but unfortunately, we are all on separate journeys. A true soulmate is a mirror, the person who shows you everything that is holding you back, the person who brings you to your own attention so you can change your life.

Pandora's Box

Pandora, in Greek mythology, was the first woman. She was created by Zeus as a counterattack when Prometheus stole fire from heaven and gave it as a blessing to mortals. Zeus had Hephaestus fashion a woman out of earth upon whom the gods bestowed their choicest gifts.

Pandora originally was depicted with a jar containing all manner of misery and evil. Zeus forgot to warn his brother Epimetheus and sent Pandora to be his wife. He opened her jar, from which the evils of misery flew out over the earth. All escaped before the lid was shut except hope.

The days that followed my appointment with the lawyer were hard to swallow. I felt horrible but knew Riley wouldn't hear why I went to a lawyer; all that would be heard was that I wanted a divorce. On Friday evening, Riley returned from Victoria. My secret made it even more uncomfortable to be around him. So I found opportunities to escape to yoga, bike rides, work—whatever I could to get away.

Saturday morning, after yoga, I had an idea to see if Riley and I could get back on track. He seems to never remember when I say something, so I thought, *What if we make a contract? Something in writing to remind him that I needed us to keep moving forward.*

I met him at one of our favourite restaurants for lunch, and he agreed to the idea. After lunch, I walked my bike next door to a used bookstore. I was drawn there but wasn't sure why. Books are heavy, and I'd have to bike them home.

I managed to pick a couple of hippy-dippy books, but I wasn't done. Cookbooks flashed through my mind. So I headed down the aisle, confused because I had gotten ride of all my cookbooks. There, in the wrong section, was a book written by Gary Chapman, the same author who had saved our marriage years earlier: *The Four Seasons of Marriage*. I had hoped to exhaust every avenue before giving the lawyer a retainer, and this was my sign that it wasn't too late.

I dove into the book, reading quotes to Riley and requesting he listen to the audio because it offered so much clarity to me. This was what I had been saying. He wasn't listening to me, but he listened to Gary's audiobook, and we became closer.

Healthy relationships are never static. They have ups and downs like every aspect of life. Things that become static become stagnant.

By Sunday evening, I was almost done with the book, but Riley hadn't even downloaded his copy. I was crushed and confronted him the next morning. He started listening, but when I headed to yoga, he stopped to do some work on my laptop. Minutes after I had gotten into the vehicle after class, Riley called to see where I was. He had been on my laptop to fix my email, and all he said was he would see me when I got home. I knew something had come from the law office by the sound of his voice.

It was a short seven-minute drive home to digest how I felt and decide what I would say. I didn't need seven minutes. I felt a weight had been lifted off my shoulders, and I knew I was going to tell my whole truth. I had finally gotten his attention.

Sure enough, it was an email from a law firm—not the one I was expecting, but it gave Riley enough of a shake that he listened to me. I told him once again how I felt. I believe he needed to see that email so he knew how serious things were and that our issues wouldn't just go away. We needed to work together, and at this point, I felt I was the only one trying.

I told him I'd booked the appointment because I was tired of guilt for not giving in and returning to his expected living arrangements. I had seen Riley grow so much over the past five years, and I reminded him of this. So I was positive he had it in him to be the partner I knew he was. Unfortunately, I was tired of being his teacher.

I didn't feel heard or appreciated for my authentic self, only as what I could offer as a mother and wife. The way he talked and treated me made me feel as if I wasn't smart enough, I couldn't do anything right. He constantly sought others' opinion over mine.

I asked for Riley to become the man I needed—my other half to support me in working toward my part of healing the world. I didn't expect him to give up his day job; I just wanted him to notice things, like the way he treated the boys as subordinates, and make adjustments.

I believe that everything is part of a bigger plan, and things happens because they are supposed to. This was our course correct, something outrageous pushing us in a different direction. I have been going with the flow, one day at a time. I am seeing the signs that our current relationship was meant to change. It created mystery when it led me to finding the right book in the wrong place. Hope was the only thing that had been keeping me where I am.

I hope for the dust to settle. I hope that things will change and improve. I hope that I just have one more challenge, and I will find bliss. When we live inside the safety of the box, we can't experience the mystery that has been let out.

Part Three
THE FUTURE

Chapter 28

THE FUTURE

Watching someone focus on their self-improvement becomes addicting! This is why so many clients eventually become friends. I want to be part of their life and growth. Their growth also motivates me to find my next opportunity to learn something new about life.

Every day at work, I see people who book with psychics looking for answers. Silly people! The future isn't written in stone. You have free will just like everyone, and we all have the opportunity for multiple different futures.

As a mom of boys, I'm pretty up-to-date on cinema superheroes. I recommend catching up on any Marvel movie with Dr. Strange to have a visual of how the future works. He travels to the future to explore the possible outcomes, and it all depends on the choices people make. When you go for a reading, the psychic is seeing what would happen if all things remain as-is and you continue down the path you are currently on. Chances are, you probably already know what they are about to tell you, because you've started to manifest it.

Through growth, you're able to expand the possible choices to create the outcome. You can't control how other people choose, thanks to free will, so to create an ideal future, one has to be open to change. Be ready to take some detours through different experiences (doors) to achieve the desired end goal. The other option is victimhood.

Everything in your life is a reflection of a choice you once made. If you want different results, make different choices.—Unknown

Both fear and love are the motivators of our decisions. Both can be used to encourage us toward or away from a choice. I've learned to fall in love with myself, and through these lessons, I know how much I truly love Riley. By allowing his family to belittle anyone in my family, I am enabling this behaviour to continue. I've watched as they have picked favourites and insulted others. Riley not standing up shows me he doesn't feel he is worthy of anything better.

Riley needs to fall in love with himself so that he knows which choice will fulfill him. For me, it's the fear of how my choice will evoke emotion in another, Riley, that has me hoping something will change and we can stay together. I know change has to happen! I love Riley and his family, but I chose to step back so they have the space to see the results of their actions.

As an empath, I feel the pain I create from my choices. I tend to suppress my desires to avoid hurting someone else. In traditional Chinese medicine, the kidneys do more than regulate the body's fluids. They also keep the opposing forces of yin and yang in balance and store the life-force energy known as *jing*. Decline is normal as we get older, but for me, I'm ahead of schedule with one kidney down and one to go. This isn't just what the Eastern medicine books say; this is what my body and soul are telling me.

The only place you'll find true happiness is within. If you looking someplace else you'll never stop searching.

In April 2022, I committed myself to a year of being open to the universe. No outside sources, in particular people telling me what

I must do to heal. I have been flowing from book to book, day to day, one foot after the other, watching and taking in what is being offered. I see a different future than I once had.

I have been grieving the future I once saw, which is now lost. I can't fix the world. I can't make other people change. I can make a choice to choose *me*, and through this choice, to thrive—showing others, spreading the magic of what growth can offer, just like the dandelion spreads its seeds.

Life's journey's not to arrive at the grave safely in a well-preserved body, but rather to skid in sideways, totally worn out, shouting "HOLY SHIT … WHAT A RIDE!"—Unknown

References

Aristotle. *Aristotle's Politics*. Oxford: Clarendon Press, 1905.

Confucius. *The Analects of Confucius: A Philosophical Translation*. New York: Ballantine Books, 1999.

Fry, Mary Elisabeth. 1932. "Do Not Stand at My Grave and Weep." (1932).

Geronimo. BrainyQuote, https://www.brainyquote.com/quotes/geronimo_198329.

Haynes, Alan. *Buddha*. New York, NY: Vertical, 2005.

Russell, Bertrand. London: Allen & Unwin.

Santayana, George. *The Life of Reason*. New York, 1905.

Usui, Mikao. 1922. *The Five Reiki Principles*.

Klaus Schwab *and* Thierry Malleret, *Covid-19: The Great Reset*. Forum Publishing, 2020

King James I, King of England, 1566-1625. (1597). *Daemonologie*, Edinburgh, Printer to the Kings Majestie.

Institoris, Heinrich, 1430-1505. (1494). Malleus maleficarum. Nurenberg: Anton Koberger.

Williamson, Marianne. "Our Greatest Fear", *A Return to Love: Reflections on the Principles of "A Course in Miracles."* (1992)

Lee Carroll *and* Jan Tober, *The Indigo Children: The New Kids Have Arrived*. United States: Hayhouse Publishing, 1999.

Barbara Ehrenreich *and* Deirdre English. *Witches, Midwives, and Nurses: A History of Women Healers*. New York: Feminist Press, 1973.

Jackson, Laura Lynne. *Signs: The Secret Language of the Universe.* Dial Press: New York, 2019.

Chapman, Gary. *The Four Seasons of Marriage.* Tyndale House Publishers, Inc. (2005)

Printed in the USA
CPSIA information can be obtained
at www.ICGtesting.com
JSHW080727170923
48577JS00004B/67

9 798765 240076